MARKETING THE SECONDARY SCHOOL

by
Brent Davies and Linda Ellison

LONGMAN

ii

Published by Longman Industry and Public Services
Management, Longman Group UK Ltd, 6th Floor, Westgate
House, The High, Harlow, Essex CM20 1YR
Telephone: Harlow (0279) 442601; Fax: Harlow (0279) 444501;
Telex: 81491 Padlog

A catalogue record for this book is available from the British Library

ISBN 0-582-08181-5

Printed and bound in Great Britain
by Bell and Bain Ltd., Glasgow

Contents

Dedication

This book is dedicated to Ray McCann.

Preface

The 1988 Education Reform Act has made schools review their management approaches and strategies in a number of areas. One of these is the way in which the school establishes an effective relationship with its clients. The term 'clients' will be used throughout this book to refer to parents, pupils and the wider community who have an involvement or interest in the school. Educationalists should not be put off by the use of such terminology as 'clients' because it is a useful shorthand for the various groups in the community which the school serves. The need for a different relationship with the external world has engendered considerable interest in marketing as both a concept and a process that can be applied to schools. Although, initially, doubts existed about the applicability of business approaches and techniques such as marketing there have been two driving forces behind the move for schools to accept the concept and to become more proactive in the marketing process.

Firstly, the increasing emphasis on more effective accountability and responsibility relationships has been noticeable for a number of years. Marketing is often seen as a coherent and comprehensive means of developing and managing those relationships. Secondly, the introduction of Local Management of Schools (LMS) and Grant Maintained Schools (GMS) has put a market dimension into the relationship between schools and their clients. As school finance is directly related to pupil numbers, the effective recruitment and retention of pupils is of vital importance to schools.

While it remains the purpose of schools to provide high quality education within a caring environment, simply providing that may not be enough. It is also necessary to be perceived as doing so and communicating that effectively. This book does not suggest that schools should be sold like 'cans of baked beans' but it does put forward an effective strategy for managing a school's reputation and allowing it to survive in a changing environment.

The book is structured so that it initially reviews the nature and dimensions of marketing and then considers how to develop a marketing culture in a school. Having established these more general management perspectives and understandings, the book then moves on to the various stages in a marketing plan. Based on the key conceptual point that marketing is a process and not a single event, the chapter outlining the marketing plan sets the scene for the following seven chapters which deal with each of the stages in this plan. They take the reader through the process of market research, analysing a school's product and service and then defining and re-defining a school's product. There follows an examination of the various promotional processes that are available and the demonstration of how all these elements can be put together in deploying a marketing strategy. The process of marketing is irrelevant if the quality of education is not maintained so that Chapter Nine looks at this central issue before the book moves on to the penultimate chapter which deals with monitoring and evaluating the marketing process itself. Finally, the conclusion puts forward an outline of the key issues for schools in this new marketing environment of the 1990s.

The book provides a basis for establishing a management perspective on marketing a school. It does not purport to be a manual on promotional tips for schools, although the promotional chapter (Chapter Seven) will provide a number of valuable insights in this area. The book demonstrates that marketing should be a serious ongoing activity for schools and one that is central to their management activity. As such it puts forward a view that there are few 'quick fixes' in marketing terms but there is a need to establish a long term marketing plan in the school. The chapters show how that plan can be initiated, developed and established.

The book is aimed at all those involved in managing secondary schools, although we believe that the basic framework and skills are equally applicable to managers in primary schools. We hope that it will play a part in enhancing the reputation of schools by demonstrating practical strategies by which they can promote the quality of the education that they offer and, thus, improve the perception of education in the world at large.

Acknowledgements

We would like to thank Dr M A Strembitsky, Superintendent of Schools, Edmonton, Canada, for permission to reproduce the questionnaires in Chapter Two. We would also like to thank the governors and senior management of Harrogate Granby High School for permission to reprint their school prospectus and flyer. We acknowledge the use in Chapter Five of the questionnaire from the Cambridge Accountability Project, 1981, Vol. 3, pp 79–80. We would also like to acknowledge the information technology skills and help of Hazel Davies.

1 The nature and dimensions of marketing

There is an increasing awareness of the need to market schools, especially within the maintained sector. This book addresses the issues which arise in the area of marketing in education and takes the reader through the management processes which are involved. This first chapter sets the context for the rest of the book by:

- defining marketing;
- demolishing some of the myths and misconceptions about marketing which have arisen in the educational world;
- examining the reasons why marketing is of increasing importance to schools;
- considering what it is that schools are marketing;
- discussing the range of clients towards whom marketing should be directed.

1. What is marketing?

Marketing is about managing relationships through effective communication. In commerce and industry it is often considered to be about managing the exchange between producers and consumers. In the educational world marketing is about *managing the relationship between schools and their clients*. A full discussion of the nature and composition of a school's clients is provided in Section Five of this chapter. Similarly, a discussion of a school's product and service is included in Section Five of Chapter Two.

Educationalists are often very suspicious of marketing because of the link with commercialism and selling. The very word seems to sum up high-powered salesmen, plastic packaging, insincerity and something slightly disreputable. Teachers often see marketing as an intrusion on educational values and feel that they should be left to their professional role of teaching children. However, it is important for schools to realise that they do not exist on an educational desert island, determining what to do and how to do it, but are accountable to the people who fund them and to the communities which they serve. All schools should already be involved in marketing because *every school has a reputation and that reputation has to be managed.*

If marketing is about managing relationships through effective communication, then that communication is, by definition, a two-way process. It is about a transaction between those who provide a product or service and those who receive it. The outcomes should be agreed and desired both by those providing education and by those receiving it. Therefore marketing in schools is not just about selling the product and service but it is about identifying the nature of what is required and then ensuring that the school gives ultimate priority to supplying that product and service and to maintaining its quality.

2. Myths and misconceptions about marketing

There are various myths and misconceptions about marketing in the educational world, one of which has been highlighted earlier, the idea that it is a rather disreputable activity. Some others are discussed in the sections which follow.

a.   That marketing is merely about promoting the school

Very often schools see marketing as designing a new school prospectus or a new school sign. These activities are, in fact, only part of one of the processes in the marketing cycle, that of promotion. What is more important for schools to realise is that the staff, and all those involved with the school, should understand the nature and dimensions of marketing as a concept.

One of the central concerns of marketing is quality. The marketing of schools involves finding out what the clients want and need (now and in the foreseeable future) and then designing a service which provides a quality education to meet those wants and needs. This is central to the idea that the concept of marketing is rooted in an organisational orientation which focuses on client wants and needs and on their satisfaction. It is concerned with the benefits derived by the customer rather than the features provided by the supplier. In essence, marketing can be seen as the key element in the accountability and responsibility relationship which the school has with its clients. The school should, therefore, effectively communicate the fact that it is providing the product/service which meets their wants and needs.

Schools should see marketing as being the way that they think about and respond to their clients and not as being a single event such as producing a brochure. The distinction has to be drawn between these single events and the overall marketing process. Marketing is thus best thought of as a *process* and not an *event*.

b. That the wants and needs of the clients are the same

The chapter will go on to discuss the various client groups that make up the 'market' of the school. Initially in this section it will use parents and children as an example to demonstrate the difference between wants and needs. There is a problem to be faced concerning the balance between the educational needs of children and the wants articulated by them or their parents. If schools are to relate their services to the wants and needs of the clients, then a dilemma may present itself because the wants as perceived by the clients may not match the pupils' needs as perceived by the professional educators.

The definition used in this book is that *wants* are things which parents and children desire or demand in terms of educational services whereas *needs* are those educational experiences and values which professional educators and society in general determine that children require at different stages of their development. Obviously, these wants and needs may not coincide at any particular moment.

If schools were to take the view that 'the customer is always right' and to try to meet the very diverse wants of individual clients, then the result would probably be a chaotic and unsatisfactory educational experience for the pupils. There are, for example, very differing views of the school's role in sex education. An alternative approach to reconciling wants and needs is required. The real art in effective management is to lead clients towards a situation where their expectations coincide with those of the school. On this basis, therefore, a school must provide an education in which content and quality both meet the needs of pupils as identified by professional educators and also satisfy the wants as identified by the pupils, parents and the local community.

This can only happen when the clients are sure that the professionals appreciate their preferences and perceptions about the nature of the educational product or service. However, it should be realised that perceptions are not fixed. They can be changed by the actions of professionals. Teachers should, therefore, be striving to assist their clients to a more sophisticated interpretation of the product or service and of the school's success criteria in line with those that they would use as professionals.

It is this view of meeting needs and wants in an accountability relationship and the effective communication of the school's values and achievements which is central to the concept of marketing. Such organisational understanding needs to precede the detailed management of the process of marketing.

c.   That either the child or the parent is the client

Having established the difference between wants and needs it is important to examine whose wants and needs are being considered. Is it the pupil or the parent who is the immediate client? The parent/child dimension of client identification is one which gives rise to a number of misconceptions and is a key issue for schools to explore. The 1988 Education Reform Act sees the parent as the 'consumer' exercising consumer rights through a policy of increased choice. However, in practice, it is not as simple as this.

In the primary school most staff would see the pupils as the clients and, therefore, the first priority of the teacher. On the other hand, secondary school teachers often consider that the parents are the clients and that they are accountable to them. This view can be considered further by assessing decisions about the choice of school. Using this as a criterion, the conclusion could be that the parent is the client when the child is younger and that the pupil becomes the client as he/she grows up. It is true that the younger the child the more dominant is the parent in making the choice of school. As children grow older and attend secondary school and, more significantly, when they move into post-16 education, they play a more dominant role in the choice process. It would be wrong, however, to take the simplistic view that the parent is the client with an increasing role being undertaken by the child as he/she grows older. At different stages and to differing degrees the child and parent influence each other as to the value and esteem in which the school is held. When the child goes home and relates good or bad experiences about the school this influences parental opinion and, in turn, the parental response influences the child's perception of the school.

While it is important to maintain an awareness of both pupil and parent wants, attention should also be focused on the deliberate transmission of positive images to the clients. This latter is a significant aspect of managing a school's reputation and is one which involves all the staff every day. Pupils should go home with a clear view of the purpose of the school and of the activities which take place so that parents feel confident about the quality of education provided. Parents should also be made aware, by more direct contact, of the school's aims and of the approaches which are being used to achieve these. If pupils and parents are committed to the school then they will reinforce each other's positive views and will act as ambassadors for the school in the wider community.

It is, therefore, necessary to reconsider the question 'Who is the client?' Perhaps it is preferable to see this not as an 'either/or' situation but as an integration of child and parental wants where a balance of interests should be met. Then, as outlined in the previous section, those wants have to be reconciled with the educational needs. Viewing both the parent and the child as the client is not fudging the issue but is the fine balance which schools must achieve in building effective relationships with their clients.

d. That marketing is concerned with selling only to people outside the school

Another misconception about marketing is that it is concerned solely with external relationships, especially the promotion of an image of the school to the outside world. It is important to realise that there are both internal and external markets and it is the internal one which needs to be given attention initially.

If those inside the school do not have a clear sense of its purpose, identity and values then it will be difficult to convince the external world of these characteristics. If individuals from the external community meet teachers, pupils and governors and perceive that they have no clear idea of what the school stands for and its successes and achievements, then it will cast doubt on the reliability of any promotional or publicity information which they have received.

In order to communicate an effective message the pupils, staff (teaching and non-teaching) and governors must have a corporate perspective. For this reason, the initial marketing activity must concentrate on those working inside the school. They need to develop a coherent view of the school, agreeing and supporting the aims and values, before any external marketing is undertaken. It is the quality of the 'internal product' that will, in the long run, effectively enhance the reputation of the school. There is little point in looking at external marketing and promotion strategies unless a coherent internal educational structure and commitment exists. In our experience many schools do exactly the opposite by concentrating on the external market first.

e. That it is 'not our job'

One of the most difficult things to change in an organisation is individuals' attitudes. It is especially difficult to change the way in which people think about marketing because of its historical development in the industrial/commercial world. Everyone inside the school, such as teachers, caretakers and secretaries, should act as ambassadors for the school and should fulfil this role when they respond to individuals or to organisations. The problem is that, too often, marketing is seen to be the sole responsibility of senior management. Traditionally, teachers have seen their job as getting on with teaching and, similarly, office staff and other support staff focus on the task in hand. However, the clients, when they assess a school, often make judgements based on the representatives whom they meet when contacting the school for the first time. This may be the school secretary who answers the telephone or the teacher whom they meet after school. It is important for all staff to see that they have a role in presenting a positive view of the school and that they should seek opportunities to do so. The traditional view of schools as being ivory towers where parents and community are kept at 'arm's length' by the professionals who guard 'knowledge and culture' does not always project a welcoming image to current or prospective clients. School signs which display 'parents are not allowed beyond this point' are not totally unknown! They say more about the organisation's view of its relationship with the outside community than any rhetoric in the school prospectus. This traditional attitude has to be replaced by one where everyone accepts that it is their task to represent and market the school.

3. Why should schools market themselves?

The need to market a school centres around both the communication of quality and the attraction and retention of pupils. Schools often believe that *'virtue brings its own reward'* but to be effective in the 1990s it is not enough simply to be a good school. What is also important is that the school is *perceived* as being a good school. The quote could be rewritten as *'virtue does not bring its own reward but virtue with a good marketing strategy may'*! Whatever the positive attributes of a school, they will not, of themselves, ensure continued success and survival unless the wider community knows about, understands and, above all, values them.

One of the prime functions of the marketing process is to ensure two-way communication between the school and its clients. The school must provide information about its aims and achievements to those who have a choice of school and also to the wider group of partners in the educational process such as industry and the local community. One aspect of this is the collection of information concerning the way in which the external world perceives the school and the expectations which are placed on it. This view is then matched with what the school can offer so that there is then a coherent information flow on which to base a promotion strategy. These processes of market research, product and service analysis and development are examined in Chapters Four, Five and Six.

Because much media attention focuses criticism on the education system, there is a great need to communicate good news in order to provide a balance. Those who work in schools know about the amount of effort that is put in and the excellent achievements of pupils. The marketing process should enable schools to display that quality. While a poor media image serves to lower the morale of teachers and deter entrants to the profession, a positive image will act as a motivating force and should also improve the quality of potential teachers. This not only applies to schools that are struggling to build their reputations but also to those which have already gained good reputations. They still need to manage the marketing process so that the reputation is protected and further enhanced. This is especially the case as other schools begin to raise their profiles in the local community.

The necessity to attract and retain pupils has been brought into sharp focus with the introduction of market forces through the 1988 Education Reform Act. The act enabled the government to continue its policy of reducing the power of monopoly suppliers, in this case the schools and the teachers, and putting power in the hands of the consumers. This is in line with a number of earlier reforms, for example, the reform of trades union legislation. In education the shift in power can be seen in terms of the very significant reduction in teacher control of the curriculum in favour of centrally determined and controlled developments in GCSE examinations and, more latterly, in the National Curriculum.

The Education Reform Act introduced Local Management of Schools (LMS) and Grant Maintained Schools (GMS) which are bringing about fundamental changes in the maintained school sector. These features, when combined with two specific aspects of the 1988 Act, formula funding and open enrolments, have a tremendous impact on the need to market a school. Formula funding has linked pupil numbers and school budgets in a direct way because the more pupils it has, the more funding a school receives. This obviously prioritises the need to attract and retain pupils. However, the effect of formula funding becomes much more dynamic when the impact of open enrolment is taken into account.

Open enrolment gives the power to parents to send a child to the school of their choice, provided that the school has the physical space to accommodate the child and that the child meets any pre-existing entrance requirements such as religious affiliation. This freedom of choice depends on two crucial factors. Firstly, there must be enough schools locally for the choice to be exercised and, secondly, the parents must have the resources (such as time and finance) to transport the child to the chosen school. Certain schools will still retain a near monopoly position because, if there are no other local schools conveniently available, parents have no effective choice. The nature of the catchment area may also mean that, even where choice exists, the convenience of a local school overcomes broader educational factors. What impact does open enrolment have on marketing a school? In this new environment, marketing to attract and retain pupils gains a much higher profile, whether schools have a near monopoly position and are only affected at the margin or whether they are in a much more competitive position.

The significance of open enrolment can be seen in Figure 1.1 which shows that increasing or decreasing pupil numbers as a result of parents operating their power of choice under the open enrolment

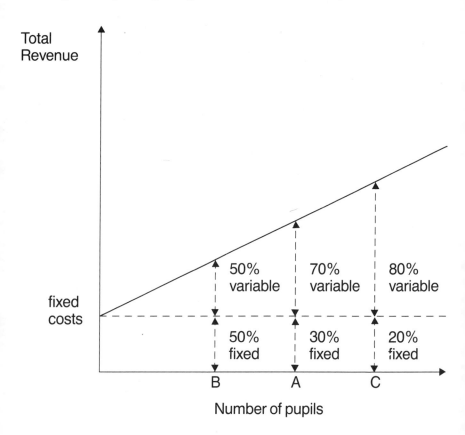

Figure 1.1   Pupil numbers and fixed and variable costs

entitlement has, through the formula funding mechanism, a direct effect on the financial viability of schools.

While this is a simplified version of the complex nature of school costs it demonstrates the impact of open enrolment and market forces on those costs.

A school at point **A** will be spending 70 per cent of its budget on variable costs such as teachers, books and equipment and 30 per cent of its budget on fixed costs (which are mainly premises-related). If it gains pupils the money which they bring in will not have to be spent on fixed costs (as the buildings are already maintained) and most of it can be spent on teachers, books and equipment. Thus, at point **C**, although the school spends the same amount on its fixed costs they are now a smaller proportion of total costs. The reverse is true when a school loses pupils. Although it receives less money it still has to meet its fixed costs. As a result these fixed costs take up a bigger share of the budget, leaving less to spend on the variable costs of teachers and materials. This can be seen at point **B** which reflects the fall in income due to a decline in pupil numbers.

Thus, with formula funding and open enrolments, the movement of pupils between schools will have a very significant effect on budgets. Expanding schools will be able to spend much of their income on teachers and materials and so attract more pupils. The reverse will be true of declining schools which will have less money but which must spend proportionately more on fixed costs. This emphasises the point that LMS and GMS are not just financial changes but that they radically alter the nature of the education system. This market mechanism has been introduced at a time when secondary rolls are low so that many schools have spare capacity and are able to draw pupils from other areas. This, of course, reinforces the need for effective marketing.

While the main reason that a school *should* be marketing is a desire to improve its service and relationship with its clients, the main reason why it *has* to market itself is that, in the 1990s, economic realities make this a precondition of its future survival. There is no point in having a quality product and having a belief that it is desirable if the message is not communicated and the school does not continue to exist.

4. What are schools marketing?

Chapter Two will discuss the nature of the product and service which the school offers while this section considers a broader perspective. Thus the discussion which follows is not just about the various values and attainments which a school puts across but it takes a different view, examining the significance of both overt and

covert performance indicators. Many schools fail to recognise the
distinction between these. Do the clients choose a school because of
its examination results and other quantifiable factors like this?
Certainly they are major factors but the reputation of a school is
made up of a series of complex and interrelated factors. Wearing
school uniform, which parents associate with good discipline, and
the amount of homework, which they associate with academic
standards, can be very significant. The reputation of many
secondary schools may be enhanced by the overt reality of good
staff – pupil relationships and high academic standards. However,
this reputation can be undone by the behaviour of pupils in the local
town at lunchtime or when travelling on school buses and by pupils
smoking outside the school gates. These determinants of the perceptions which parents have of the school are often more important than
the reality of what is actually going on in the delivery of effective
education.

A useful management exercise for school staff to undertake is to
list four strengths and weaknesses of the school as they perceive
them (an exercise which is described in Chapter Five). Then they
should draw on the knowledge from the interaction which they have,
for example, with parents at parents' meetings in order to list the
strengths and weaknesses as perceived by parents. The key management information comes in comparing the two lists. It is not only the
teachers in the school who set the criteria; there may be significant
factors in the perceptions of parents which determine the reputation
of a school but which have little to do with its core educational
activities.

Schools, therefore, have to consider whether they are concentrating on marketing a set of values which parents take for granted
but are ignoring a number of factors which parents perceive as being
key indicators of a 'good' school. While the authors would not
suggest that fundamental educational values are ignored at the
expense of marketing pragmatism, it is vital that staff do not assume
that they know what parents regard as significant indicators of a
school's success. If they are to fulfil their educational mission,
schools must address the concerns of their clients and respond to
them. The only way to do this is to sample parental opinion to find
out what is considered to be significant rather than to rely on the
existing teacher perceptions based within the internal culture of the
school.

However, any response to client wants must be a genuine one.
The image projected must reflect the product and service which a
school actually delivers. If a false view is conveyed, it will not be long
before the various client groups will realise that they have been
misled.

5. To whom are schools marketing?

If marketing a school centres on the concept of effective communication, then it is vital to have a clear view of the target audience. A simplistic view would be to look only at the immediate consumer, the parent or child, especially when one considers the implications of formula funding and open enrolment. However, this approach ignores the broader set of clients who are, for a variety of reasons, also significant in marketing terms.

Schools do not exist to provide teachers with jobs; they exist to provide effective education for their clients. It is, therefore, an essential prerequisite for the effective marketing of schools that staff should reflect on the nature and dimensions of client groups. Market segmentation is a way of dividing clients and potential clients into groups within which there are identical needs. However, because of the diversity of expectations from the education service, it would be more realistic to consider that the clients in a segment would have broadly similar, rather than identical needs. If this concept of market segmentation is applied to schools, the following grouping could result:

Internal Markets:
- Governors
- Staff (teaching and non-teaching)
- Regular visitors and helpers
- Current pupils
- Current parents

External Markets:
- Prospective parents and pupils
- Prospective staff
- Other educational institutions
- The local community
- Commerce and industry
- The Local Education Authority
- National groups and organisations

The importance of effective communication with each of these market segments will be outlined below and then methods of promotion will be explored later, in Chapter Seven.

Internal markets

(i) *Governors* need to play an active role in the management of the school if they are to understand the school and to be committed to achieving its aims. Increasingly, governors are realising that this is a difficult and time-consuming task. They will only be able to play an effective and informed role in managing and marketing a school if they work in partnership with the senior management team.

(ii)   Staff (teaching and non-teaching)   As was explained earlier, it is important that these internal partners in the education process have a clear view of the aims of the school and the policies for achieving these aims. Senior management should help all staff to realise that they each have an important part to play in managing the school's reputation as they implement these policies and in their communications with those outside the school's traditional boundary.

(iii)   Regular visitors and helpers may only be in the school for a short time so it is especially important that they can quickly recognise that quality and commitment are being combined to give effective education for the pupils. It is all too easy for such visitors to leave with a biased, unfavourable view of a school based on an isolated incident. Care should be taken to ensure that they are given relevant and positive information to take with them to the external environment.

(iv)   Current pupils can be key ambassadors because they carry both explicit and implicit messages about the school as they move around in the community. Through positive reinforcement they need to be made aware of the school's aims and its achievements so that they can communicate an effective message.

(v)   Current parents of existing pupils are a very important client group. It is obviously desirable to maintain their support so that these current pupils remain in the school but it should not be forgotten that there may also be younger children to follow. Parents make a choice to send a child to the school. If they perceive that the child is receiving a 'good' education and if that fact is being communicated to them, then they will be satisfied with what they are receiving. Schools should ensure that parents have their original choice reaffirmed by effective positive communication about the school and about their child's progress.

Of equal importance is the fact that parents are very often the key influence-makers in the local community. They can act as ambassadors for the school to the external market, ie friends, colleagues and neighbours with children. However, dissatisfied parents may move their child to another school. Few parents go to that extreme but what they do is to express dissatisfaction to friends and neighbours locally who will be persuaded against choosing the school. This is the latent effect of parental influence: it may not be noticed immediately and may take two or three years to work through.

It is important to ensure that existing parents have a clear and positive view of the school, not only to develop their understanding of the product and service which they are receiving but, through them, to build the school's reputation and intake in the future.

External markets

(i) Prospective parents and pupils The need to attract new clients, from both within and outside the traditional catchment area of the school, is one of the main reasons why many schools first begin to explore the concept of marketing. It is the attraction of new clients that ensures the continuing success of the school. There is an increasing awareness amongst parents of the existence of a choice mechanism so schools must be ready to respond positively to requests from them for information or for visits to the school.

Herein also lies one of the major professional objections to the marketing of schools — the idea of 'poaching' pupils from fellow professionals. It is to be hoped that the approach to marketing which is outlined in this book, ie the management of a school's reputation through the communication of a 'quality' message, will help to counter these objections.

(ii) Prospective staff There are well documented cases of schools being unable to recruit either the quality or quantity of staff which is desirable, especially in certain subjects and geographical areas. It is therefore important to communicate a clear and positive picture of the school to prospective staff so that they apply for and accept posts which are offered.

One of the key dimensions here is whether or not the existing staff speak highly of the school when they talk to colleagues. There may be a 'staffroom mafia' which provides a cynical view of the school to potential colleagues; if so this needs to be countered. There are various factors which a school must address. What arrangements are made for advertising, interviewing and appointing staff? What are staffroom facilities like? How helpful are secretarial and support staff when prospective staff telephone the school? What coherent staff development policies are available so that staff can extend their skills and knowledge, and hence their effectiveness, in the future? Would staff recommend a colleague to work there? What messages do they give when they meet professional colleagues at meetings or conferences, especially in the bar afterwards? In an era of increasing staff shortage these factors can be critical in establishing a 'good reputation' for the school as an employer and retainer of staff.

(iii) Other educational institutions Most of the pupils who enter a
secondary school will have been to local primary schools. The view of
the secondary school which is held by the parents, pupils and staff at
the primary school can be critical to the decisions which both parents
and pupils make. Parents and primary school staff should be convinced
that there is true continuity and progression between the two sectors.
The historical primary – secondary divide has to be broken down and
reinterpreted as a total package of educational provision from four to
eighteen. People can only be convinced that this is so if the reality is
reflected in the working relationships between the different partners
in the education service. A secondary school with a Sixth Form needs
to market this provision to other secondary schools whose pupils might
transfer in at sixteen. This will help to ensure the viability of its own
provision.

A school's reputation with Further and Higher Education Institutions is more complex. When considering places for school leavers, the
range of possible destinations is so great that concentrating on a limited
number with whom to forge close links may be the best strategy. If
relationships are good, local universities, polytechnics and colleges can
provide valuable services such as the use of facilities and support for
teaching staff in the form of teaching practice students or guest lecturers.
It is worth remembering that universities, colleges and polytechnics
also need students. They will see schools as clients and will be anxious
to help and to build links.

(iv) The local community members contribute (through local and
central government taxes) to the funding of state education. As many
schools know to their cost, local reputations take a long time to build
but are very quickly lost. It is important, therefore, to maintain a
positive image within the community. However, the individuals within
that community are very diverse and have different perceptions of what
a school should be so that it is difficult to satisfy everyone. It is necessary
to target key people with influence locally and to ensure that they are
kept informed of school developments and involved in appropriate
activities. For example, local councillors may be useful in linking in
with the Local Education Authority.

There are often key points where the school comes into contact with
the community such as on the buses taking pupils home after school.
The behaviour of pupils here may be more critical in determining the
school's reputation than more formal interactions. Key points such as
this need careful monitoring.

(v) Commerce and industry For a variety of reasons, it is important
to market the school to local businesses and to associated liaison groups
such as the Chamber of Commerce. Industry and commerce usually

have a view of the quality of education in a school. This may be based on hearsay but it will affect the availability of jobs for pupils. For demographic reasons, employers may not be able to have such a wide choice of school leavers in the future but this does not mean that schools can become complacent. An ever increasing percentage of pupils are now taking part in work experience schemes and the availability of quality placements will depend on the employers' perceptions of the school (and of its pupils). If a school has marketed itself well and has a good reputation, then it will be much easier to have involvement with commerce and industry for careers advice, staff development and enterprise schemes. Sponsorship (usually in the form of goods or services in kind) may well be available to those schools which best communicate the quality message. Local and national businesses have their own reputations to protect so it is unlikely that they will wish to be associated with badly managed schools which are not meeting the needs of the pupils. Good relationships could enhance the promotional process because, when new employees move into the area, they will be told of a school's reputation and may choose it for their children.

(vi) The Local Education Authority (LEA) is an important stakeholder because it is providing funds so that the school can function. It is, therefore, a client of the school with the school undertaking to provide a number of places and educational provision on behalf of the LEA. A further dimension to this relationship is the fact that parents who are looking at school availability will often approach the LEA for information. It is thus incumbent upon the school to communicate the quality of its work to all officers of the LEA, especially to those who deal with parental enquiries. They need to be fully aware of the school's aims and special features.

Although the power and responsibility of the LEA has been reduced since the Education Reform Act, it still retains an inspectorial role and some discretionary funds. Interestingly, the LEA is also a provider in that the school will 'buy' services from the LEA and, thus, the relationship is two-way. Even Grant Maintained Schools which have opted out of LEA control have to retain effective links for some aspects of local organisation.

(vii) National groups and organisations   There has, since 1976, been an ongoing debate about educational standards in state schools. One way of counteracting the extensive coverage given to poor standards is to market the schools in a very positive way to Central Government, local MPs and, through the media, to the country as a whole.

Various specially funded projects (such as TVEI) take place in schools and care should be taken at all levels to ensure that such funding continues. The availability of specific grants and various types of sponsorship will depend on the providers' perceptions of the 'value for money' which results from the investment.

Members of Her Majesty's Inspectorate (HMI) make different types of visits to schools. On each occasion they should receive a clear marketing message — that a quality product is being delivered and that quality control is part of the everyday operation of the school.

Conclusion

This initial chapter has sought to establish a management overview of marketing within an educational context. While later chapters will explore the approaches which can be employed at various stages in the process, such tactical activities can be undertaken only when this strategic view is understood by the various participants.

The reader should now have a clear view of the nature of marketing. The next chapter addresses the key management task of attitude change: how to establish a marketing culture in a school. Once this has been considered the book moves on to designing and implementing an effective cycle of activity in the marketing of a school.

2 Developing a marketing culture in a school

The most difficult part of marketing a school is not necessarily just adapting or operationalising the key stages in the school marketing plan but it is the establishment of a marketing culture within the school. It is important to examine some of the critical concepts in moving the attitude of management and staff from being product-orientated to being more client-orientated. In order to be more effective, this organisational understanding must precede the detailed management of the marketing process. The chapter is organised into seven sections which focus on the issues in the development of this client-orientated philosophy:

1. The importance of the client
2. Responding to clients
3. Never letting the client down
4. One impression of the school or many?
5. Ensuring that the school provides a service as well as a product
6. Managing a high quality service approach
7. Developing a new philosophy

1. The importance of the client

The previous chapter discussed client identification in education, examining the pupil/parent relationship and the concept of the wider community as a client of the school. The way that clients have to date been perceived by schools may be considerably different from the way that a commercial or industrial company would think of a client. While in the business world the idea of being client-orientated or of putting the customer first is commonplace, such an attitude can seem somewhat out of place in education. The culture of schools has traditionally centred on being the source of knowledge and transmitting this to a captive audience. The result has been a product-orientation where knowledge and skills have predominated. Much can, however, be learned from commerce and industry. Raising these issues and applying some of the business concepts can provide a useful stimulus to start the educational debate concerning the ways in which we think about clients.

Here are a number of statements which should provoke discussion:

1. The client is the most important person in the school and the quality of the contact, in person, in writing or by telephone is the key to a successful relationship.
2. A client comes to us for education; we should provide this in a way (the service) that delivers a professional product which satisfies both the wants and needs of the client.
3. The client is not something that is additional to the school: without the client there is no school.
4. Clients do not interrupt our work; they are our work.
5. Whereas the client may be dependent on us for providing an education, we are dependent on the client for our jobs.

This sort of thinking is quite powerful if used with staff groups so that they can address the way in which they perceive clients and the importance of client relationships to the organisation. Such challenges to existing patterns of thinking are necessary in order to move schools into becoming market-orientated. This book does not propose that we should forget the traditional values of schools in favour of just considering clients' wants but argues very strongly that the knowledge and skills in the schools should be orientated so that they meet not only those wants, but also the identified needs of the clients. This means that we must rethink our view of the client and adopt a client-orientation. The school and the client are not separate, the clients are part of the school if not the school.

2. Responding to clients

Clients expect to be treated seriously, courteously, with concern and with problem-solving rather than blame-attaching attitudes. In industry, staff at all levels would undertake training on how to deal with clients on a face-to-face basis and on the telephone but in education we are usually left to learn by 'trial and error'. Developing experience this way has, on the majority of occasions, worked quite well but there are exceptions. When it does not there are problems with the trial and error approach — it can be a *trial* for the client because we make *errors*!

A good example of how we treat clients is provided by examining what happens when the telephone is answered. Is the response, 'Good morning, Brentwich School, can I help you?' or is it just a curt 'Yes!'? Do we respond 'the headteacher is working with children and we always give that priority in this school but she will telephone you later' or 'the headteacher's wandering around the school as usual, can you try later?'

Another example is found in the management of parents' meetings. How do we train teachers to communicate with parents so that the teacher's expectations and parents' expectations meet and both go away satisfied with the encounter? The truth is that we spend little or, more often, no time in thinking of training staff in meeting the clients' expectations and handling the communication exchange with them.

Clients expect their problems to be solved and not to be told that there are so many internal procedures which prevent a solution. While, in the real world, it is not possible to meet the often contradictory wants of different groups of parents, the *attitude* with which staff tackle the problems and look for positive solutions is often the factor which parents remember. This is the perspective that must be developed in staff if an effective marketing culture is to be established.

3. Never letting the client down

Do not promise what you cannot deliver and make sure that you deliver what you promise! Parents do not expect miracles or exceptional service but they do expect consistent, good quality education and, above all, that the school should honour its promises. If it promises homework on a Tuesday night and there is none, the school has failed a performance indicator which it set itself. Similarly, if it promises to respond to parents' letters within a week, then it should honour that obligation. Performance indicators which you set for yourself are the ones that, if broken, do the most damage to your reputation. Similarly, pupils who are promised visits that do not take place or hand in work for marking which is not returned on time (or even not marked at all) will have a broken promise and may develop negative attitudes.

There have been many instances in which parents have attended
parents' meetings and been told that the teacher does not like any
children to get too far ahead in their work. This implies that the
teacher is unable to cater for the needs of the individuals in a class.
Parents will soon pass such messages on to their friends and acquain-
tances and the school will develop a poor reputation.

All these activities emphasise two points:

1. the importance of clients in the eyes of the providers — if
   they have low priority or esteem they will be let down
   because it is not felt to be important to keep promises;
2. the need to develop a strong consensus in the clients' collective opinion of the effectiveness of the school.

4. One impression of the school or many?

It is often said that 'first impressions count' and that the first
impression which a client has of a school, for example the entrance
hall or a friendly greeting from the school secretary, is critical. This
is undoubtedly true but another perspective is that clients make up
their view of a school through a series of factors which, although
individually insignificant, aggregate to give a very powerful message
about the school. Such factors could be the quality of the newsletter,
the telephone manner of the staff, the length of time it takes to
respond to a letter or the quality of the organisation of the parents'
meeting; all are contact points which either portray competence and
care or incompetence and indifference. It is sometimes hard to convince staff that an activity such as offering a parent a cup of tea at
a meeting can be critical in developing an opinion about the school.
In themselves such factors are very trivial but, when aggregated,
they can form a chain of impressions about an individual member of
staff or the school.

The message for schools is that all staff should be aware that
every exchange with clients, no matter how insignificant it may seem
at the time, may be critical in the chain of events which forms a
client's opinion of an institution.

5. Ensuring that the school provides a service as
well as a product

One of the great traditions of education in the UK is that it has
always been regarded by its proponents at national and local level as
an education *service*. We are not just in the business of providing a

one-dimensional product such as examination results but a much broader approach which educates the whole person. If this is the case, we should focus much more on that service and how it is perceived rather than just on the product. For example, when teaching a particular subject, the teacher is not just in the information transfer business, teaching the material and then going away. What he or she is involved in is a much more sophisticated and complex relationship with the child which focuses on other aspects of the child's development. The successful teacher shows that he or she recognises the individuality of the class members and values that individuality. It is aspects of the hidden curriculum such as caring relationships, encouragement and equality of opportunity which are important in developing the whole child. These factors and attitudes also give positive messages to parents about the school's approach to their children. Teachers, therefore, have to recognise and internalise these values not just because they are sound educational practice but because this 'service' element is a critical performance indicator for the school from the client's perspective.

Another example of this product-orientation which neglects the wider service aspects is provided by teachers who become obsessed with product activities such as routine marking, assessment, reports or form filling and neglect the key role in a people-orientated activity — relating to their clients. Such routines should never be allowed to become purely administrative and mechanistic chores. The feedback which a pupil receives on a piece of work or a term or a year's work should be part of the process of development and improvement. General comments such as 'Good' or, even worse, 'Could do better' do not indicate a caring attitude. Clients expect useful feedback and the priority that is given to this aspect demonstrates the values and approaches of the school.

6. Managing a high quality service approach

A management priority in all organisations should be to adopt a client-orientation, focusing on the development of a high quality service approach. However, this is particularly difficult to achieve in an educational context for four reasons and these factors should receive significant management attention.

1. When the educational product or service is being delivered to the client, whether it is a lesson for a child in the classroom or a conversation with a parent at a parents' meeting, the interaction is outside the direct control of the school's management.

2. Once the educational service has been delivered there is very little that is tangible. The way in which an interaction is perceived determines how the quality of the school will be recognised. Thus the clients will *perceive* that they have (or have not) received a quality service in terms of a good lesson or a successful interview. This transitory interaction is, therefore, highly significant in assessing quality from a client's perspective. The significance of such interactions needs to be reinforced within the school.

3. Although it is important to assess the quality of the whole educational experience, it is difficult for school management to monitor attitudes; attention has focused in the past on monitoring and evaluating educational processes. The ways in which staff are perceived and the pupils' views of the school have not traditionally received the same level of attention as these educational processes. A good example of how perceptions can be investigated is provided by the *Edmonton Attitude Survey* questionnaire, part of which is reproduced at the end of this chapter. Management should take steps to seriously evaluate perceptions as well as the product.

4. There are many personnel with whom clients may come into contact. Wherever possible clients should deal with as few people as possible. They should be able to identify and relate to key individuals and not be passed around the organisation from person to person. They can then form strong positive relationships with the key person who represents the school to them.

So how do we manage this high quality service approach? The key to success in this is defining standards and ways of dealing with clients that are developed and agreed by staff so that they have ownership of the concepts. Time will be needed for this policy development process. Time is also needed in order to undertake the necessary staff development so that all are aware of how to adopt a high quality service approach. There must also be a management framework to monitor the quality of the delivery of the product and service. Many schools have experimented with 'pupil tracking' as a monitoring device. This involves following one pupil through a week to analyze the quality of the educational experience received. This approach can be extended to observe other types of interaction, for example with parents. There should also be a regular reappraisal of how communications work, for example how enquiries are dealt with, in order to ensure that the system does not defeat its intent.

7. Developing a new philosophy

It is necessary to challenge the whole way in which we traditionally perceive schools and to construct a new philosophy about how we think about them. A fundamental approach in response to this challenge to the existing perception of schools is to reconsider the way we think about clients by asking the question, 'What are the assets of the school?' The traditional answer in accounting terms would be the buildings, the classrooms, desks, chairs and equipment. In human relations terms the answer would be the staff because they undertake the educational process. These have always been misconceptions; schools are not of much use to society if they have furniture and teachers but have no children to be taught. They then become a waste of society's resources. A more fundamental analysis would establish that all these assets, both human and physical, only facilitate the education process. The key ingredient is the pupils themselves. Within the school a similar perspective can exist. For example, the school librarian may consider a 'good' library as one with tidy desks and chairs and neat rows of books which fill the shelves, whereas the most effective library may be the one where children are sitting everywhere reading and the books, therefore, are off the shelves being used. So it is with whole schools. They do not exist to provide neat tidy buildings or jobs for teachers; they exist for the children and for their education. This has been brought into sharp relief with the advent of formula-based funding associated with Local Management of Schools and Grant Maintained Schools. In this new framework empty chairs and desks are liabilities rather than assets. Rooms still have to be insured, cleaned, heated and other fixed costs met despite there being fewer pupils in the class. The real assets are the pupils and the parents who send them to the school. Without the pupils nothing else is possible; all the other components only facilitate the education process once this vital asset is in place.

This is a different, but necessary, way of thinking about the assets of the school. Organisations such as local government and the civil service have often been pilloried for being bureaucratic and more concerned with rules and regulations rather than with the people whom they serve. The structures and ways of working are not an end in themselves but merely a means of achieving a quality of service to a customer. So it is in schools; all the buildings, organisational structures and staff only exist to provide the client with quality education. We should not, therefore, lose sight of this when organising the resources which deliver education.

Schools must stop being inward looking and dealing only with the day-to-day problems and challenges of the teaching process.

They must consider the fundamental importance of the client in the school and how the recipients of education, their parents and the wider community, view the school. Management in schools needs to encourage this development of attitudes about the centrality of the client and to create significant management opportunities for promoting this way of thinking.

Conclusion

This chapter has built on Chapter One by moving away from defining the nature of marketing to challenging the traditional ways of thinking in order to establish a marketing culture in the school. These two chapters combine to provide the background analysis and perceptions which are needed before the practical stages in the marketing cycle can be undertaken. The next chapter sets out that practical marketing plan by putting forward a cycle of activity that can take place once this basic understanding has been established.

Figure 2.1   *Edmonton Attitude Survey* Questionnaires

1990 7-9 STUDENT SURVEY

We would like to know how you feel about school. Please check the box
which best describes your feelings about the following:

	I'm Satisfied	I'm dissatisfied	I'm Not Sure
1. The number of complementary courses open to you			
2. The usefulness of your courses			
3. The emphasis on basic skills (such as reading, writing, mathematics)			
4. Your homework assignments			
5. How much you are learning			
6. How the marks are determined to indicate your performance in school courses			
7. What the school tells your parents about how you are doing in school			
8. Your principal			
9. Your assistant principal (answer only if there is one)			
10. The office staff			
11. Your teachers			
12. Your counselor			
13. High school and career planning assistance			
14. The say that you have in school decisions that affect you			
15. The way student discipline is handled			
16. The behaviour of other students in class			
17. The behaviour of other students out of class			
18. School rules and regulations			
19. The way other students treat you			
20. How attendance problems are handled			
21. The opportunity to get into classes that you would like			
22. Lunch arrangements			
23. The extracurricular program (sports, school plays, concerts, clubs, etc.)			
24. The students' union or council			
25. The school buildings, grounds and equipment			
26. The interest that your teachers have in you			
27. The opportunity for experiencing success in your programs			
28. The number of students in your classes			
29. The length of your class periods			
30. The services of the school library or learning resources centre			
31. The cleanliness of your school			
32. Your school in general			
33. The information that you receive in the school about what you are expected to learn			
34. The challenge provided for you by your school programs or courses			
35. The way your achievement is recognized			

PLEASE USE OTHER SIDE OF THIS QUESTIONNAIRE FOR YOUR COMMENTS

EDMONTON PUBLIC SCHOOLS

1990 10-12 STUDENT SURVEY

We would like to know how you feel about school. Please check the box which best describes your feelings about the following:

	I'M SATISFIED	I'M DISSATISFIED	I'M NOT SURE
1. The number of option courses open to you			
2. The usefulness of your courses			
3. The emphasis on basic skills (such as reading, writing, mathematics)			
4. Your homework assignments			
5. How much you are learning			
6. How the marks are determined to indicate your performance in school courses			
7. What the school tells your parents about how you are doing in school			
8. Your principal			
9. Your assistant principal(s) or coordinator(s) (answer only if there is one)			
10. The office staff			
11. Your teachers			
12. The counselors			
13. Further education and-or career planning assistance			
14. The say that you have in school decisions that affect you			
15. The way student discipline is handled			
16. The behaviour of other students in class			
17. The behaviour of other students out of class			
18. School rules and regulations			
19. The way other students treat you			
20. How attendance problems are handled			
21. The opportunity to get into classes that you would like			
22. Lunch arrangements			
23. The extracurricular program (sports, school plays, concerts, clubs, etc.)			
24. The students' union or council			
25. The school buildings, grounds and equipment			
26. Help in planning your high school program			
27. The interest that your teachers have in you			
28. The opportunity for experiencing success in your programs			
29. The number of students in your classes			
30. The length of your class periods			
31. The services of the school library or learning resources centre			
32. The cleanliness of your school			
33. Your school in general			
34. The organization of the school year (semester, 10 month, etc.)			
35. The information that you receive in the school about what you are expected to learn			
36. The challenge provided for you by your school programs or courses			
37. The way your achievement is recognized			

PLEASE USE OTHER SIDE OF THIS QUESTIONNAIRE FOR YOUR COMMENTS

EDMONTON PUBLIC SCHOOLS

1989 PARENT SURVEY

Edmonton Public Schools would like your views...
Your responses will be treated with complete confidentiality. Please use the attached prepaid envelope for returning your completed questionnaire
Your responses should relate specifically to your child named on the envelope in which you received this questionnaire and to the school identified in the box below.
Thank you - your participation is very much appreciated. For assistance or clarification please call Ian Wilson, Assistant Superintendent Information.
429-8440

JUNIOR HIGH

FOR EACH ITEM BELOW PLACE A CHECK MARK IN THE APPROPRIATE BOX ACCORDING TO HOW YOU FEEL ABOUT THE QUESTION

		YES	NO	NOT SURE
1	Do you feel that the school district is offering and emphasizing the right programs of studies for students?			
2	Do you feel that you are being adequately informed about the school's programs and accomplishments?			
3	Do you feel that you are being adequately informed about the school district's programs and accomplishments?			
4	Are you satisfied with the information provided by the school about what your child is expected to learn ?			
5	Are you satisfied with the information provided by the school about how your child is expected to behave?			
6	Do you feel that your child is sufficiently challenged by the school to foster maximum learning and development?			
7	Are you satisfied with your involvement in activities or programs at your child's school?			
8	Are you satisfied with your involvement in the budget planning process at your child's school?			
9	Do you feel student discipline is being handled well at the school?			
10	Do you feel your child likes school?			
11	Do you feel the school district is using its money in a reasonable manner?			
12	In general are you satisfied with: a) your child's teacher(s)?			
	b) the school principal?			
	c) the associate superintendent of schools for your area?			
	d) the superintendent of schools?			
	e) the board of trustees?			
13	Do you feel welcome at the school?			
14	Do you feel you have an adequate voice in school decisions that affect your child?			
15	Do you feel you are being satisfactorily informed about your child's learning progress?			
16	Are you satisfied with the guidance and counseling services at the school?			
17	Are you satisfied with the extracurricular programs at the school (sports, school plays, concerts, clubs, etc.)?			
18	Are you satisfied with the way attendance is handled at the school?			
19	Do you feel the non-teaching staff at the school such as secretaries, aides and custodians, are helpful and friendly?			
20	Do you feel that the number of students in your child's classes is appropriate?			
21	Do you feel that your child's school experiences are consistent with the values taught in your home?			
22	Are you satisfied with the library services at your child's school ?			
23	Are you satisfied with the cleanliness of your child's school ?			
24	Generally, are you satisfied with your child's school ?			
25	Are you satisfied with the arrangements for children who wish to have lunch at school?			
26	Are you satisfied with the assistance provided by the school to you and your child in planning for high school and career?			

Is there anything you would like to communicate to the board or administration?
PLEASE USE OTHER SIDE OF THIS QUESTIONNAIRE FOR YOUR COMMENTS.

 EDMONTON PUBLIC SCHOOLS

COMMENTS

The questionnaire responses and the information that you have provided in the comments below will be treated with full confidentiality.

_____
_____
_____
_____
_____
_____
_____
_____
_____
_____
_____
_____
_____
_____
_____
_____
_____
_____
_____
_____
_____
_____
_____

••

REQUEST FOR DIRECT RESPONSE

If you have any comments or concerns to which you would like a direct response please list them in the space below. You should also provide a telephone number or address at which you may be contacted. A response will be provided to you before September 30, 1989.

_____
_____
_____
_____
_____
_____
_____
_____
_____

1989 PARENT SURVEY

Edmonton Public Schools would like your views...
Your responses will be treated with complete confidentiality. Please use the attached prepaid envelope for returning your completed questionnaire
Your responses should relate specifically to your child named on the envelope in which you received this questionnaire and to the school identified in the box below.
Thank you - your participation is very much appreciated. For assistance or clarification please call Ian Wilson Assistant Superintendent Information, 429-8440

	SENIOR HIGH	YES	NO	NOT SURE
	FOR EACH ITEM BELOW PLACE A CHECK MARK IN THE APPROPRIATE BOX ACCORDING TO HOW YOU FEEL ABOUT THE QUESTION			
1	Do you feel that the school district is offering and emphasizing the right programs of studies for students?			
2	Do you feel that you are being adequately informed about the school's programs and accomplishments?			
3	Do you feel that you are being adequately informed about the school district's programs and accomplishments?			
4	Are you satisfied with the information provided by the school about what your child is expected to learn ?			
5	Are you satisfied with the information provided by the school about how your child is expected to behave?			
6	Do you feel that your child is sufficiently challenged by the school to foster maximum learning and development?			
7	Are you satisfied with your involvement in activities or programs at your child's school?			
8	Are you satisfied with your involvement in the budget planning process at your child's school?			
9	Do you feel student discipline is being handled well at the school?			
10	Do you feel your child likes school?			
11	Do you feel the school district is using its money in a reasonable manner?			
12	In general are you satisfied with: a) your child's teacher(s)?			
	b) the school principal?			
	c) the associate superintendent of schools for your area?			
	d) the superintendent of schools?			
	e) the board of trustees?			
13	Do you feel welcome at the school?			
14	Do you feel you have an adequate voice in school decisions that affect your child?			
15	Do you feel you are being satisfactorily informed about your child's learning progress?			
16	Are you satisfied with the guidance and counseling services at the school?			
17	Are you satisfied with the extracurricular programs at the school (sports, school plays, concerts, clubs, etc.)?			
18	Are you satisfied with the way attendance is handled at the school?			
19	Do you feel the non-teaching staff at the school such as secretaries, aides and custodians, are helpful and friendly?			
20	Do you feel that the number of students in your child's classes is appropriate?			
21	Do you feel that your child's school experiences are consistent with the values taught in your home?			
22	Are you satisfied with the library services at your child's school ?			
23	Are you satisfied with the cleanliness of your child's school ?			
24	Generally, are you satisfied with your child's school ?			
25	Are you satisfied with the arrangements for children who wish to have lunch at school?			
26	Are you satisfied with the assistance provided by the school to you and your child in planning for high school and career?			
27	Are you satisfied with the number of course choices open to your child?			
28	Do you feel the school provides appropriate programs for students not intending to continue their schooling beyond high school?			
29	Do you feel that the length of your child's class periods is appropriate?			

Is there anything you would like to communicate to the board or administration?
PLEASE USE OTHER SIDE OF THIS QUESTIONNAIRE FOR YOUR COMMENTS.  EDMONTON PUBLIC SCHOOLS

COMMENTS

The questionnaire responses and the information that you have provided in the comments below will be treated with full confidentiality.

_____
_____
_____
_____
_____
_____
_____
_____
_____
_____
_____
_____
_____
_____
_____
_____
_____
_____
_____
_____
_____
_____
_____
_____

• •

REQUEST FOR DIRECT RESPONSE

If you have any comments or concerns to which you would like a direct response please list them in the space below. You should also provide a telephone number or address at which you may be contacted. A response will be provided to you before September 30, 1989.

_____
_____
_____
_____
_____
_____
_____
_____
_____

1990 TEACHING STAFF SURVEY

The board of trustees, the superintendent of schools and your administration would like to know your feelings about Edmonton Public Schools as a place to work. Please help us by completing this questionnaire, sealing it in the accompanying envelope, and returning it to the proper representative for your school or department. Questionnaires will be sent to us without any individual identification. The reports produced will contain ONLY group statistical summaries and anonymous comments, with no identification of individual respondents.

Thank you for your help.

FOR EACH QUESTION BELOW PLACE AN "X" IN THE APPROPRIATE BOX ACCORDING TO HOW YOU FEEL ABOUT THE QUESTION.

	VERY MUCH	FAIRLY MUCH	NOT VERY MUCH	VIRTUALLY NOT AT ALL
1. Do you feel there is good communication throughout the school district?				
2. Do you feel there is good communication in your school?				
3. Are you satisfied with the staff performance evaluation process in your school?				
4. Do you feel you as an individual have adequate influence over district level decisions that affect you and your job?				
5. Do you feel you as an individual have adequate influence over school level decisions that affect you and your job?				
6. Do you feel you get support when you need it from: a) the associate superintendent for your area?				
b) the superintendent of schools?				
*c) your principal? (SEE NOTE BELOW)				
7. Do you feel you get adequate recognition and appreciation for your performance and accomplishments?				
8. Do you feel your assigned work responsibilities are fair and reasonable?				
9. Do you feel that the district is compensating you fairly?				
10. Do you feel that the school district's goals, philosophies and policies are communicated clearly?				
11. Do you feel that the school district's goals, philosophies and policies are implemented consistently?				
12. Do you feel that the school district's goals, philosophies and practices are consistent with your personal goals and beliefs?				
13. Do you have respect and confidence in: a) the associate superintendent for your area?				
b) the superintendent of schools?				
c) central services?				
d) the board of trustees?				
e) Alberta Education?				
* f) your principal? (SEE NOTE BELOW)				
14. Do you feel that the promotion of staff within the school district is fair and reasonable?				
15. Do you feel that the school district is a good place to work?				
16. Do you feel that your school is a good place to work?				
17. Are you satisfied with your involvement in the budget planning process?				
18. Do you feel that you have adequate opportunities for professional development?				
19. Are you satisfied with the support provided by central services?				
20. Do you feel that the workload in the school is distributed equitably and fairly among staff?				
21. Do you feel that the number of students in the classes that you teach is appropriate?				
22. Are you satisfied with the parental involvement in educational activities and programs provided at your school?				
23. Are you satisfied with the involvement of the non-parent community in educational activities and programs at your school?				
24. Do you feel that sufficient information is provided to the students about what they are expected to learn?				
25. Do you feel that sufficient information is provided to the students about how they are expected to behave?				
26. Do you feel that sufficient information is provided to parents about what their children are expected to learn?				
27. Do you feel that sufficient information is provided to the parents about how their children are expected to behave?				
28. Do you feel that the school is providing sufficient challenging opportunities for students to experience success in the school programs?				

PLEASE USE THE OTHER SIDE OF THIS QUESTIONNAIRE FOR YOUR COMMENTS

EDMONTON PUBLIC SCHOOLS

*NOTE: QUESTION 6(c), 13 (f) - TEACHING STAFF ANSWER ON STAFF SURVEY - PAGE 2 ONLY

1990 TEACHING STAFF SURVEY – PAGE 2

FOR EACH QUESTION BELOW PLACE AN "X" IN THE APPROPRIATE BOX ACCORDING TO HOW
YOU FEEL ABOUT THE QUESTION.

	VERY MUCH	FAIRLY MUCH	NOT VERY MUCH	VIRTUALLY NOT AT ALL
6. c) Do you feel you get adequate support when you need it from your principal?				
13. f) Do you feel you have respect and confidence in your principal?				

EDMONTON PUBLIC SCHOOLS

1990 SCHOOL SUPPORT STAFF SURVEY

The board of trustees, the superintendent of schools and your administration would like to know your feelings about Edmonton Public Schools as a place to work. Please help us by completing this questionnaire, sealing it in the accompanying envelope, and returning it to the proper representative for your school or department. Questionnaires will be sent to us without any individual identification. The reports produced will contain ONLY group statistical summaries and anonymous comments, with no identification of individual respondents. Thank you for your help.

FOR EACH QUESTION BELOW PLACE AN "X" IN THE APPROPRIATE BOX ACCORDING TO HOW YOU FEEL ABOUT THE QUESTION.

	VERY MUCH	FAIRLY MUCH	NOT VERY MUCH	VIRTUALLY NOT AT ALL
1. Do you feel there is good communication throughout the school district?				
2. Do you feel there is good communication in your school?				
3. Are you satisfied with the staff performance evaluation process in your school?				
4. Do you feel you as an individual have adequate influence over district level decisions that affect you and your job?				
5. Do you feel you as an individual have adequate influence over school level decisions that affect you and your job?				
6. Do you feel you get support when you need it from: a) the associate superintendent for your area?				
b) the superintendent of schools?				
c) your principal?				
7. Do you feel you get adequate recognition and appreciation for your performance and accomplishments?				
8. Do you feel your assigned work responsibilities are fair and reasonable?				
9. Do you feel that the district is compensating you fairly?				
10. Do you feel that the school district's goals, philosophies and policies are communicated clearly?				
11. Do you feel that the school district's goals, philosophies and policies are implemented consistently?				
12. Do you feel that the school district's goals, philosophies and practices are consistent with your personal goals and beliefs?				
13. Do you have respect and confidence in: a) the associate superintendent for your area?				
b) the superintendent of schools?				
c) central services?				
d) the board of trustees?				
e) Alberta Education?				
f) your principal?				
14. Do you feel that the promotion of staff within the school district is fair and reasonable?				
15. Do you feel that the school district is a good place to work?				
16. Do you feel that your school is a good place to work?				
17. Are you satisfied with your involvement in the budget planning process?				
18. Do you feel that you have adequate opportunities for professional development?				
19. Are you satisfied with the support provided by central services?				
20. Do you feel that the workload in the school is distributed equitably and fairly among staff?				

PLEASE USE THE OTHER SIDE OF THIS QUESTIONNAIRE FOR YOUR COMMENTS.

EDMONTON PUBLIC SCHOOLS

1990 SCHOOL CUSTODIAL STAFF SURVEY

The board of trustees, the superintendent of schools and your administration would like to know your feelings about Edmonton Public Schools as a place to work. Please help us by completing this questionnaire, sealing it in the accompanying envelope, and returning it to the proper representative for your school or department. Questionnaires will be sent to us without any individual identification. The reports produced will contain ONLY group statistical summaries and anonymous comments, with no identification of individual respondents. Thank you for your help.

FOR EACH QUESTION BELOW PLACE AN "X" IN THE APPROPRIATE BOX ACCORDING TO HOW YOU FEEL ABOUT THE QUESTION.

	VERY MUCH	FAIRLY MUCH	NOT VERY MUCH	VIRTUALLY NOT AT ALL
1. Do you feel there is good communication throughout the school district?				
2. Do you feel there is good communication in your school?				
3. Are you satisfied with the staff performance evaluation process in your school?				
4. Do you feel you as an individual have adequate influence over district level decisions that affect you and your job?				
5. Do you feel you as an individual have adequate influence over school level decisions that affect you and your job?				
6. Do you feel you get support when you need it from: a) the associate superintendent for your area?				
b) the superintendent of schools?				
c) your principal?				
7. Do you feel you get adequate recognition and appreciation for your performance and accomplishments?				
8. Do you feel your assigned work responsibilities are fair and reasonable?				
9. Do you feel that the district is compensating you fairly?				
10. Do you feel that the school district's goals, philosophies and policies are communicated clearly?				
11. Do you feel that the school district's goals, philosophies and policies are implemented consistently?				
12. Do you feel that the school district's goals, philosophies and practices are consistent with your personal goals and beliefs?				
13. Do you have respect and confidence in: a) the associate superintendent for your area?				
b) the superintendent of schools?				
c) central services?				
d) the board of trustees?				
e) Alberta Education?				
f) your principal?				
14. Do you feel that the promotion of staff within the school district is fair and reasonable?				
15. Do you feel that the school district is a good place to work?				
16. Do you feel that your school is a good place to work?				
17. Are you satisfied with your involvement in the budget planning process?				
18. Do you feel that you have adequate opportunities for professional development?				
19. Are you satisfied with the support provided by central services?				
20. Do you feel that the workload in the school is distributed equitably and fairly among staff?				

PLEASE USE THE OTHER SIDE OF THIS QUESTIONNAIRE FOR YOUR COMMENTS.

EDMONTON PUBLIC SCHOOLS

1990 PRINCIPAL SURVEY

The board of trustees, the superintendent of schools and your administration would like to know your feelings about Edmonton Public Schools as a place to work. Please help us by completing this questionnaire, sealing it in the accompanying stamped envelope, and returning it through regular Canada Post services. Completed questionnaires should not have any individual identification. The reports produced will contain ONLY group statistical summaries and anonymous comments, with no identification of individual respondents.

Thank you for your help.

FOR EACH QUESTION BELOW PLACE AN "X" IN THE APPROPRIATE BOX ACCORDING TO HOW YOU FEEL ABOUT THE QUESTION.

AREA 1

	VERY MUCH	FAIRLY MUCH	NOT VERY MUCH	VIRTUALLY NOT AT ALL
1. Do you feel there is good communication throughout the school district?				
2. Do you feel there is good communication in your school?				
3. Are you satisfied with the staff performance evaluation process in your school?				
4. Do you feel you as an individual have adequate influence over district level decisions that affect you and your job?				
5. Do you feel you as an individual have adequate influence over school level decisions that affect you and your job?				
6. Do you feel you get support when you need it from: a) the associate superintendent for your area?				
b) the superintendent of schools?				
7. Do you feel you get adequate recognition and appreciation for your performance and accomplishments?				
8. Do you feel your assigned work responsibilities are fair and reasonable?				
9. Do you feel that the district is compensating you fairly?				
10. Do you feel that the school district's goals, philosophies and policies are communicated clearly?				
11. Do you feel that the school district's goals, philosophies and policies are implemented consistently?				
12. Do you feel that the school district's goals, philosophies and practices are consistent with your personal goals and beliefs?				
13. Do you have respect and confidence in: a) the associate superintendent for your area?				
b) the superintendent of schools?				
c) central services?				
d) the board of trustees?				
e) Alberta Education?				
14. Do you feel that the promotion of staff within the school district is fair and reasonable?				
15. Do you feel that the school district is a good place to work?				
16. Do you feel that your school is a good place to work?				
17. Are you satisfied with the budget planning process?				
18. Do you feel that you have adequate opportunities for professional development?				
19. Are you satisfied with the support provided by central services?				
20. Do you feel that the workload in the school is distributed equitably and fairly among staff?				
21. Do you feel that the number of students in the classes that you teach is appropriate?				
22. Are you satisfied with the parental involvement in educational activities and programs provided at your school?				
23. Are you satisfied with the involvement of the non-parent community in educational activities and programs at your school?				
24. Do you feel that sufficient information is provided to the students about what they are expected to learn?				
25. Do you feel that sufficient information is provided to the students about how they are expected to behave?				
26. Do you feel that sufficient information is provided to parents about what their children are expected to learn?				
27. Do you feel that sufficient information is provided to the parents about how their children are expected to behave?				
28. Do you feel that the school is providing sufficient challenging opportunities for students to experience success in the school programs?				

PLEASE USE THE OTHER SIDE OF THIS QUESTIONNAIRE FOR YOUR COMMENTS

 EDMONTON PUBLIC SCHOOLS

3 Establishing a marketing plan

This section of the book concentrates on the way in which schools can establish an effective marketing plan. The first thing to realise is that there is no simple technique, such as producing a new prospectus or similar promotional material, which will prove to be effective in anything other than the short term if it is used in isolation from a coherent marketing plan. If the plan is to be effective in building a positive relationship between a school and the community which it serves then it needs to be built up over a period of time to encompass all the stages of the marketing cycle.

It is important, at this initial stage, to decide who will oversee the development and implementation of the marketing plan. Senior management must have a strategic involvement because they have the organisational vision about where the school is going. Whether the senior management take operational responsibility for the marketing plan is an issue that they will have to consider carefully. Many schools are now designating a member of staff as a marketing officer to manage the process, working with a marketing group or committee. Governors are increasingly wishing to be involved in such groups and, indeed, there is often a marketing subcommittee of the governing body although we would not necessarily advocate this latter approach unless staff were to be extensively involved in it.

To reinforce a point made earlier in the book, it is a mistake to consider marketing as a single event. Instead it should be considered as a process with a number of stages that contribute to the overall plan. This marketing plan can be represented as a cycle of activity as in Figure 3.1.

The purpose of the plan is to ensure that those responsible for marketing in the school go through each of the stages in the marketing cycle and do not just focus on one particular activity. The first stage is *market research* which establishes what the clients want

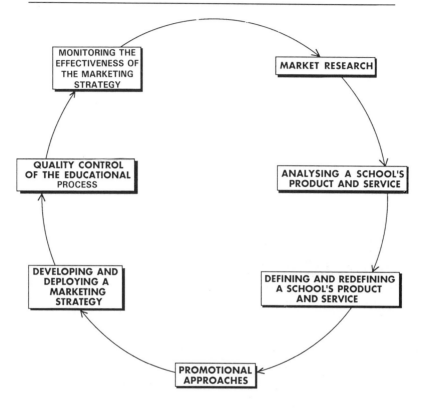

Figure 3.1 The marketing cycle

and need from the school and reviews the environment in which the school operates. Having established this, an examination must be made of what the school has to offer and the clients' perceptions of this product and service. This is achieved in the second stage, that of *analysing the school's product and service*.

Having established the *wants and needs of the market* and *what the school has to offer*, the third stage is to *define or redefine the school's product and service*. This third stage is vital in ensuring that a clear message emerges concerning how the school is to meet or reconcile the needs and wants of the market with what the school has to offer. It will then be necessary to examine various *promotional approaches and techniques* that are available to communicate the information about the school. Then, and only then, can the school move on to the fifth stage, that of *developing and deploying a marketing strategy*.

Here management must consider who is to be involved and how and which strategies should be employed.

The two final stages involve checking quality. The sixth stage is concerned with making sure that the product that is being delivered, 'quality education', is what it purports to be and that it is perceived as such by the client. This *quality control of the educational process* is at the heart of all good schools. It is also at the heart of marketing because, in the long run, you can only market a good product. The seventh and final stage is the *monitoring and evaluation of the marketing process*. Here the efficiency and effectiveness of the marketing effort is reviewed.

It can be seen that marketing has seven important stages and needs to be viewed as a process with individual stages seen in that context. A clear message to reinforce to all colleagues is that marketing is a continuous *process* and not a single *event*. The way in which schools can undertake each of the stages will be the focus of the succeeding chapters.

4 Market research

Market research is concerned with gathering information. This is necessary in the marketing process because it is neither desirable nor effective for those in a school to base their decisions about client wants and needs on personal assumptions. Nor is it desirable to make assumptions, merely on personal opinions, about the suitability of the present educational product or service. Such assumptions can be inaccurate and misleading; what is needed is objective information. Through the process of market research schools can carry out an audit which collects factual data about the clients and the educational environment and about the school as it is currently perceived. Market research is, therefore, the starting point of the marketing process because it provides the information on which all subsequent decisions and activities are based. This chapter examines six key questions concerning the process of market research:

1. What is market research?
2. Why should schools undertake market research?
3. What do schools need to find out?
4. When should schools carry out market research?
5. Who should carry out market research?
6. How should schools carry out market research?

Because this field of data collection is very large, for the convenience of the reader, we have divided the practical aspects between this chapter and Chapter Five. In this chapter we have focused on practical techniques for gathering information on the school's environment, on client expectations and on the identification of pupil needs. Chapter Five examines techniques which focus more specifically on clients' perceptions of the product and service offered and provides practical examples. Both chapters should therefore be seen as an entity, separated only for convenience of presentation.

1. What is market research?

Market research is the systematic collection and analysis of information which relates to the school and the environment in which it is operating. More specifically, *it is a means of qualifying and quantifying the nature of client wants and needs and of monitoring the school's effectiveness in satisfying those wants and needs.* It is, therefore, concerned with gathering information from both internal and external sources.

2. Why should schools undertake market research?

A school carries out market research in order to acquire information on which to base its decision making about strategies for effective interaction with its clients. It undertakes this, firstly, in order to fulfil its accountability responsibilities more accurately and completely and, secondly, in an open enrolment environment, to provide information which is vital at one level for survival and at another level for expansion. Market research should therefore supply information which forms the basis for decision making about the nature and quality of the product and service to be provided and about effective and efficient strategies for marketing that product and service.

3. What do schools need to find out?

The process of market research should enable the school to obtain specific information about the following four broad areas:

- the school's environment
- client expectations
- the educational needs of the pupils
- client perceptions of the product and service.

(i) The school's environment

It is important to be aware of the local and national context in which the school is operating. Market research should therefore:

- identify local and national trends which impact on the school and its context such as employment patterns, legislation, the effect of pressure groups, national politics, educational change. This is often referred to as a PEST or STEP analysis which considers political, economic, social and technical factors;

- identify the clients and potential clients (using the broader view of client definition given in Chapter One). The school should identify its total market, the significant segments in this market, its catchment area and the actual clients. Attention should focus on identifying elements of the internal as well as the external market. It is important to assess not only the current position but also to identify potential changes and trends that may result in new or alternative segments which can be exploited in the future;
- examine the behaviour and actions of clients. How do clients hear about the school? How could relationships with potential clients be developed? When do they choose it or develop links with it? This information will help the school to target promotion at key times of the year and in particular locations;
- examine the potential for growth — what is the potential to expand the provision which the school is offering? Is this provision purely to be seen as educational or is the school able to broaden its services, for example by starting foreign language courses for commerce and industry?
- identify any evidence of potential decline — what is happening and why and, most significantly, can any decline be reversed by changing the school's emphasis?
- identify resource/income generation potential — what opportunities are there to expand the school's financial and other resources?
- identify the competitors — who are the school's major competitors now? Who is likely to be a major competitor in the future?
- monitor the activities, successes and failures of other schools (locally and nationally).

(ii) Client expectations

In order to be fully informed about what the clients want the school must:

- identify clients' present wants — in terms of the nature and quality of the product and service;
- identify the anticipated wants of the present clients and of the potential clients.

The school can then use this information when redeveloping and promoting its product and service.

(iii)   *Educational needs of the pupils*

It was explained earlier that, while it is important to be responsive
to client wants, schools should take account of the educational needs
of pupils as defined by the professional educators. Market research
should gather data to:

- identify the present needs of pupils in the school;
- identify the future needs of the current pupils and of those
  who may enrol, for example the needs as defined by the
  National Curriculum legislation and the examination boards.

(iv)   *Clients' perceptions*

The various client groups can provide information about their
perceptions of the school and the wider educational service. This will
enable the school to:

- examine its image, ie the clients' views of the general strengths
  and weaknesses of the school. The clients in the various
  market segments (including the teaching staff) will have
  different views which may have to be reconciled if one
  corporate image of the school is to be projected;
- identify a wide range of views concerning the potential
  opportunities and threats that may be presented in the future;
- monitor client satisfaction with specific aspects of the present
  provision. How satisfied are current pupils and parents about
  specific aspects of the curriculum? How effective are
  home – school links and communications? What is the effectiveness of the newsletter?
- monitor the public perception of the quality of the educational product and the service. How do employers perceive
  children who come from the school?
- assess changes in the attitudes to the school of the clients in
  each segment;
- monitor market awareness and attitude — how much
  awareness, knowledge and interest is there in each market
  segment concerning the school and its activities? This will
  help the school to monitor its current marketing approaches;
- identify the clients' perceptions of other schools, especially
  its competitors.

A fuller analysis of investigating client expectations is undertaken in
Chapter Five.

4. When should schools carry out market research?

Market research should always precede the other activities in the marketing cycle. However, it need not be seen as a daunting task which takes place at a fixed point in every school year. There may be occasions when there needs to be a major focus on market research, for example:

- if there has been no market research carried out in the past;
- if it is felt that major changes in the external environment may not have been fully assessed by the school.

At other times, the school should use market research as an ongoing forecasting and monitoring device which takes place alongside other activities. There are many opportunities to make contact with the school's clients at events such as parents' meetings, open days/ evenings and careers conventions. These events can also be followed up by contacting a representative sample of those attending in order to gather information about their perceptions of the events themselves. Some schools make a point of telephoning a few parents at random each week to monitor their general satisfaction with the school and its activities. This tends to identify minor grumbles about which the parents would not bother to contact the school but that could, potentially, escalate and damage the school's reputation in the future.

5. Who should carry out market research?

Each school will have to work out its own way of determining who will undertake the market research. What follows is a series of questions to which each school will need an answer.

- Who will collect and analyse the information? Will this be left to individuals or a team of people? How senior will they be? Will such a team be limited to school staff or should it extend to include parents, governors, pupils and the wider community?
- Will interim progress reports be required? To whom will the researchers report back? What are the powers and responsibilities of the team undertaking the market research?

It is necessary to clarify these issues before starting the market research activity otherwise confusion about roles and responsibilities will ensue.

6. How should schools carry out market research?

Just as it is important not to launch into a publicity campaign
without first going through the earlier stages in the marketing cycle,
so it is equally important that market research, as the first stage in
that cycle, should not begin without careful preparation. Before
rushing into market research those responsible must consider the
process involved in market research and then work systematically
through that process. This avoids starting at the midpoint with a
number of misapprehensions and then having to backtrack. For
example, it is important to decide the precise data required so that
the managers will be supplied with adequate information to make
effective decisions. The market research process can be divided into
the four stages outlined in Figure 4.1.

Stage one — identifying information needs

The senior management in a school should have a clear view about
the decisions that are to be made so that they can identify the
information which must be acquired through market research in

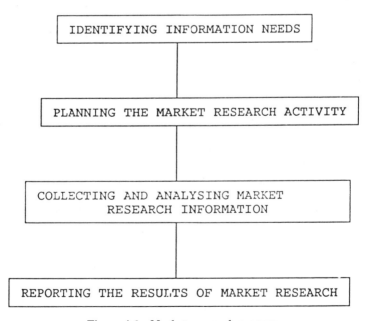

Figure 4.1 Market research process

order to make those decisions. The decisions will fall into one of two groups, either being about the *strategic context* in which the school operates or about more *specific situations* or problems at the tactical level.

Strategic decisions will require information concerned with the broad educational environment but may also necessitate information on trends concerning client expectations, needs and perceptions. An example of this change in the strategic context would be the impact on parental opinion and on subsequent recruitment trends of a neighbouring school achieving grant-maintained status.

As well as strategic marketing questions there may be some specific issues which have arisen from previous research into broad areas or from a reactive response to a problem that the school is experiencing. Each fairly narrow problem must be identified and clarified before the market research process begins. For decision making at this tactical level, the information required will be more focused but could be in any of the four areas identified on page 40. A school would, for example, seek opinions from parents in a very specific way about possible changes in school uniform policy and uniform design. Thus, Stage One, the establishment of a clear view of the school's precise problem or need for information, will help to focus the market research and save time and resources. The following example demonstrates the importance of this focusing down of the market research effort in order to clarify the precise nature of the investigation. Decisions may be required within the broad area of home—school links but, before any market research begins, there will need to be a much clearer focus on the elements of that area. There could be a case in which a school feels that low attendance at parents' meetings is caused by the unappealing nature of the events. In fact, the problem might be the timing of the events or the poor communication about their purpose. In either case, it would be pointless looking for ways of merely making the meetings more attractive. The danger is that, because the initial focus of the investigation was inadequate, the school could expend a great deal of time and effort to obtain a large amount of confusing information.

Stage two − planning the market research

Having identified the decision area and the information needed, it is then necessary to determine how to gather that information and how it might be analysed. For this to be done effectively, a structured approach is required. The school must go through a number of key questions concerning the framework within which the market research must operate. These questions will focus on:

- the sources of the information
- the approaches to be used to obtain the information
- the resources available.

(i) Information sources The key to success in effective market research is in assessing potential sources of information. These may be secondary or primary sources. *Secondary* information is so called because it is already available somewhere, having previously been collected for another purpose. *Primary* information, on the other hand, is gathered specifically for the task in hand. No matter how the information is obtained, it should be evaluated to check that it is relevant, accurate, up-to-date and impartial.

Secondary information is already in existence, either within the school or in the external environment. Researchers usually start by examining this because it can be obtained relatively quickly and cheaply. For example, data about each child (such as ability, medical conditions, address and travelling distance to the school) may be kept on individual files but the data are not always aggregated in a useful way. In this case the researcher has to search through and sort material in existence rather than collecting new data. Useful secondary sources would be as follows:

(a) Internal information
The wealth of existing school documentation can be utilised if it is re-sorted. Curriculum information, timetables, pupil records, assessment profiles and staff records are examples of data that are collected for a specific purpose but which, when re-sorted and combined with other data, may provide valuable information to aid decision-making in a different management area. A simple, but very significant, source is the pupils' work. If, for example, each pupil, during the first term after transfer from a feeder/partner primary or middle school, is asked to write an essay about his or her likes, dislikes, hopes and fears in the new school, then there will be a wealth of information. It will be possible to see how the school is perceived, how that perception agrees with reality and how successful the school has been in managing the transfer and creating a view in the pupils' and parents' eyes of a caring, effective school. Unfortunately, such information normally remains in the pupils' exercise books and is not used in a corporate manner. There are many other examples of information that is not aggregated in a useful way to form a broader picture. Evaluation undertaken by individual departments or year groups can feed information into a whole school review. Letters from parents and other

clients which may be treated as isolated items can, if correlated, form an integrated picture. Inspection reports from LEA advisers/inspectors and from HMI are another source of information waiting to be used.

(b) Central and local government documentation
- National Curriculum materials
- Assessment and testing regulations and guidance
- Education Acts and circulars
- LEA policy statements
- Local planning information eg industrial and housing development proposals
- Regional statistics eg on birth rate, unemployment

This type of documentation is the basis for much of the research into pupils' present and future needs, especially in an era of central determination of the curriculum. It also provides a lot of information on the local and national environment.

(c) Books, journals and the media
These sources will give information about the environment in which the school currently operates but they are especially valuable in providing ideas and information for strategic planning.

(d) Miscellaneous sources
- Pressure group press and publication releases
- Exhibitions — including other schools' open events
- Other schools' documentation
- Educational and other databanks
- Professional associations

Although these sources may prove useful, it is from these wider areas that excessive, unfocused information may be gathered. Care should therefore be taken to use it selectively.

It may well be that secondary data cannot provide all the information that is needed to solve a particular problem. Often, more specialised information is needed. If this is the case, the school will have to undertake its own collection of original data from primary sources.

Primary information is gathered specifically for the problem under investigation. A typical example would be a questionnaire to ascertain parental opinion on an issue. This type of information is likely to be more costly and time-consuming to acquire than secondary information because the researchers have to create the data as well as sorting and interpreting it. Before collecting primary data it will be necessary to consider the possible research approaches and to decide which one(s) will be used in order to obtain the information.

(ii)   Research approaches   Depending on the information required, the choice will probably be between observation and survey methods. *Observation research* can be considered to be observing relevant people, actions and situations. This is a useful method for collecting information that people are unwilling or unable to provide. A good example would be undertaking research to check the quality of the school by:

- telephoning the school to check the quality of response
- sending for a school brochure
- acting as a prospective parent
- assessing ease of use of bus routes, parking and the buildings
- walking around the neighbourhood to assess general conditions and the environment

However, the observations, unless repeated several times, may not give an adequate sample on which to base major decisions although they do provide useful indicators for a more in-depth follow-up. The main drawbacks of this method are the time which may be required to carry it out and the fact that it may have to be carried out at a specific time.

Survey research can be considered to be the gathering of descriptive information. This is the most widely used method of finding people's knowledge, attitudes, preferences and choice patterns. Typically, this approach uses questionnaires and interviews and has either:

- a structured approach — with formal lists and all the people being 'processed' in the same way

or

- an unstructured approach — with the researcher probing and guiding according to response.

One of the advantages of the survey approach is that it provides the flexibility to obtain many kinds of information in many different situations. It can be quicker than observational research. However, it has several disadvantages. People are sometimes unwilling to answer or have no time to respond. They may be tempted to give an answer even if they do not really know or they may be tempted to give an answer designed to please or deliberately to mislead. The method of contact used depends to a certain extent on the size of the research sample, on the research instrument and on resource constraints such as time, cost and opportunity for contact. Suitable methods include:

Mail — by using postal questionnaires, large amounts of data can be collected relatively cheaply. It is often thought that this method elicits more honest replies and eliminates interviewer bias. It does, however, require simple questions if standardised responses are to be obtained because it is not possible for the researcher to explain the questions to the respondent. The limitations of the method are that it takes time to receive the responses and often there is a poor response rate. It also has the limitation that the sender or recipient cannot develop answers from the predetermined structure and that anyone may complete the questionnaire — not necessarily the person for whom it was intended.

Telephone — this approach ensures that the school can target the required individual. It has the advantages that it is quick and easy and the interviewer can explain the questions as necessary. It also allows the interviewer to develop the material and to respond to questions. There is usually a good response rate but there may be problems of cost and there is the possibility of bias in asking questions and recording answers.

Personal — a very effective way of obtaining information from individuals or groups is to meet them face-to-face. Using structured or unstructured interviews, this approach gives an in-depth opportunity to collect original data. The main disadvantages are the time taken (and therefore the cost) and interviewer bias. The advantages are that the interviewer can achieve a good response rate, knows that the right person is giving the responses and can develop points. This activity can be undertaken, for example, at parents' meetings or on industrial visits.

(iii) Resources There will, inevitably, be resource implications when market research is being carried out. Staff will have to devote *time* to the exercise and some *materials* will be needed. Consideration must be given to the *quality* of the resources eg the skills which are available, whether or not the individual or team will require some training and, if so, where that might be available.

When the planning of market research is complete, the proposals should be approved by senior management before implementation. The aims and objectives should be clearly stated, along with the strategies for achieving these. Once they have given their approval to the market research approach, senior managers must be committed to resourcing that approach. They must determine the timespan of the exercise so that the results of the research can lead into the decision making process at the appropriate point.

Stage three — collecting and analysing market research information

Once Stage One (Identifying Information Needs) and Stage Two (Planning the Market Research Activity) have been completed, the process of collecting and analysing the information can take place. Having defined the purpose, approach and tactics the hard work begins. Often older pupils can undertake this collection and analysis as part of their studies as well as the marketing group undertaking its own activities.

Stage four — reporting the results of market research

When interpreting and reporting findings it is important to make sure that the report:

- is precise
- is written in clear, simple language
- gives a summary as well as detailed findings
- is focused on the needs of the decision-makers
- is focused on what can be achieved.

Conclusion

It can be seen from this chapter that market research is the first key stage in the marketing cycle and that it involves finding out what the clients want and need and exploring the educational environment. An examination of the way in which this information conflicts or is reconciled with the school's existing educational product and service is a major management task. Thus, the next chapter will consider how a school can 'analyse its product and service'. Chapter Six will bring together these two perspectives in the third stage of the cycle, 'defining and redefining a school's product and service'.

If the reader wishes to pursue and apply the issues raised in this chapter, the following exercises provide a framework to do so.

Chapter four: exercise one

Identifying your market segments

Market segmentation was defined in Chapter One as a way of dividing clients into groups with similar needs.

A.   Study the following market segments from Chapter One. With your own school in mind, add new ones (including those which might offer potential in the future) and delete any which are inappropriate.

Internal Markets:
- Governors
- Staff (teaching and non-teaching)
- Regular visitors and helpers
- Current pupils
- Current parents

External Markets:
- Prospective parents and pupils
- Prospective staff
- Other educational institutions
- The local community
- Commerce and industry
- The Local Education Authority
- National bodies

B.   Examine each of these segments in turn and decide:
1. have its wants ever been investigated by your school?
2. has it been the focus of marketing activity in the past by your school?

C.   Choose the six segments upon which the marketing process might best focus. This should enable the school to target its strategy so that maximum effectiveness is achieved.

Chapter four: exercise two

The internal market

The importance of the internal clients is stressed throughout this book. This exercise focuses on the significance of these clients as ambassadors of the school.

Consider each of the clients below.

Assess the value of each group as ambassadors of the school using the following scale:

1. Very significant
2. Significant
3. Insignificant

Internal targets   *Value*
  (i) **Governors**
       (you may wish to subdivide by type)

 (ii) **Teaching staff**
       (you may wish to subdivide by type)

(iii) **Non-teaching staff**
       ● Clerical
       ● Technical
       ● Caretaking
       ● Cleaning
       ● Lunchtime supervisors

 (iv) **Regular visitors and helpers**
       (it is helpful to list the various types)

  (v) **Current pupils**
       Year 7
       Year 8 and 9
       Year 10 and 11
       Year 12 and 13

 (vi) **Current parents**

(vii) **Others**
       (list types)

Chapter four: exercise three

The pupil recruitment area

The questions asked here will become more significant as parents increasingly exercise their rights under open enrolment legislation. If the information is to be used effectively, it is important to gather specific data, especially in response to question D.

A. Where is the school's traditional recruitment area?

B. How many pupils out of this traditional area attend competing schools?

C. How many pupils have you recruited recently from outside this traditional area?

D. What are the reasons for these shifts in recruitment patterns?

Chapter four: exercise four

Hearing about the school

This exercise allows the school to examine customer behaviour by investigating the ways in which they hear about the school. It also looks at the school's mechanisms for monitoring this information.

A. Compile a list of the most common ways in which parents hear about the school and its reputation.

    (If there is no record of this you could use a postal questionnaire, sending it to all parents of the pupils in the first two year groups.)

B. How do you monitor how the parents find out about the school in the first place?

    Does the school secretary ask when they telephone?

    Are they asked when they visit the school?

    Is the question on any documents which are sent to the parents of new children?

Chapter four: exercise five

Income generation potential

Although many schools are seeking to broaden their resource base, others see a cut in expenditure, rather than a boost to income, as the only way to 'balance the books'. Because of the effect of formula funding, the most significant benefits are obtained if more pupils can be recruited. While it is often difficult to obtain sums of money, there are many other resources which can be obtained, especially locally, if the school manages its reputation effectively.

A. Use the following matrix to identify potential resource providers and the resources which they can supply.

Resource/Providers	advice	skills	money	equipment	materials	time
Local industry/commerce						
Parents and grandparents						
Local community						
LEA						
District or county council (eg libraries, museums, the emergency services)						
Further education						
Higher education						

B. In the first column list each of the areas in the matrix which represent a significant resource gain to the school. In the second column list the activities which currently help to promote the school to that particular client group.

....	....
....	....
....	....
....	....
....	....
....	....

Chapter four: exercise six

Parent and child expectations

The following sheet assesses parent and child expectations
of the school. It could easily be adapted to cover other client
groups.

    A. PARENTS
        What do parents want from the school?

    B. PUPILS
        What are the pupils' wants and expectations from
        the school?

    C. How do the two sets of information differ?

Chapter four: exercise seven

The professionals' views of pupil needs

This exercise considers the general attributes which a pupil
should possess when leaving the school.
   Ask the teaching staff the following questions:

What skills should the child have acquired by the time
he or she leaves the school?

What qualities should the school be developing in each
child?

What   standards   of   behaviour   are   desirable?

C

Chapter four: exercise eight

The national expectation

The following questions are intended to focus attention on
more specific areas of the school's activity than those in
exercise seven.

A. What are the main qualities that pupils should
    display in order to be employable?

B. What experiences do pupils need in order to become
    valuable members of society?

---

5 Analysing a school's product and service

The analysis of a school's product and service can be considered as part of market research in that it is part of the process of obtaining information for decision making. It requires that the perceptions of the various clients are examined. However, there is value from a management perspective in assessing the *environment* and *what the market wants and needs* as one stage (in Chapter Four) and then assessing the *perceptions* of what the school has to offer as a second stage (this chapter). This makes it much clearer for the school's managers to operate: they can reflect on the two sets of information and define the educational product and service to be provided (Chapter Six). A school needs to identify *what* it is offering currently before it can reinforce or adapt that to the marketing challenges which it faces.

This chapter will focus on examining perceptions of what the school currently provides for its clients. The problem in identifying what the school has to offer centres on assessing the exact nature of the current product and service. This relies on people's perception of what exists. For example, if the strengths of the school are being considered then different people's perceptions (governors, head, staff, pupils) may give a very different picture of what the school is offering. The range of perceptions of the school's existing provision can be obtained by investigating the views of the various client groups. This can then be added to the evaluation of the school and its activities by professionals in order to provide an integrated assessment. There are various approaches and techniques available for gathering and analysing perceptions of what the school is offering. This chapter will concentrate on three approaches which can be used:

1. A SWOT analysis (strengths, weaknesses opportunities, and threats);

2. General questionnaires and interviews;
3. Specific professional evaluation instruments such as
    Guidelines for Review and Internal Development in Schools
    (GRIDS) used internally by the school or external profes-
    sional assessments provided by the LEA or HMI.

The first two approaches could be used with any of the school's
clients but the instruments encompassed in the third are designed
for use by professional educators within the school. The rest of this
chapter examines these approaches and gives examples of their use.

1. A SWOT analysis

In the commercial/industrial world significant use is made of a
SWOT (strengths, weaknesses, opportunities and threats) analysis.
As the name suggests, it focuses on key aspects of an organisation.
This approach is increasingly being used in the public sector and, in
particular, in the educational world. It is normally aimed at the
whole school level but it can easily be applied at a sub group level,
such as a department or year group. A SWOT analysis is straightforward to carry out because it just involves compiling four lists. It
can be undertaken by a variety of people — teachers, senior management, non-teaching staff, governors, pupils, parents etc. If the
SWOT analysis originates from the teaching staff, it is better if the
other partners are *asked* for their perceptions rather than simply
having assumptions made about the way in which they might view
the school. Figure 5.1 is a typical SWOT form layout that can be
used in a school. The form can be completed in several ways to
obtain the necessary information. Staff can be asked to fill it in on
an individual basis, recording their personal opinions of the school's
strengths, weaknesses, opportunities and threats. This information
can then be collated by senior management. An improved process
would be to ask staff to share their views once the initial form has
been completed. In groups they could articulate individual perceptions and, perhaps, come to a group consensus. This could then be
fed to senior management to give a whole school perspective. When
it comes to assessing other clients' perspectives, either the staff can
give their view of how these are similar or different *or*, better still,
actual sampling of client opinion can take place with parents, pupils
and the wider community being asked to give their views on the four
areas. The key task of the senior management team in the school is
to pull these various pieces of information together to form a clear
management view as a basis for action. The following sections give
a detailed description of each of the elements in the SWOT analysis.

	STAFF PERCEPTIONS	CLIENT PERCEPTIONS
STRENGTHS		
WEAKNESSES		
OPPORTUNITIES		
THREATS		

Figure 5.1 SWOT form layout

After this, an exemplar as in Figure 5.2 is provided of a completed
SWOT analysis for a typical secondary school.

Strengths

These are, as the name suggest, the things which the school or area
does well. Teachers often find it difficult (owing to inbuilt modesty)
to articulate their own individual strengths but, in our experience,
they are more ready to state school, department or year group
strengths. The school may take it for granted that it has a good
academic record and cares for its pupils. Do the teachers articulate
that perspective and do parents and other clients recognise it? For
example, if the exam pass rate for GCSE is above the national
average, do all the staff know? Do they know by how much? Has
this been communicated to the pupils and to other clients?

Having identified certain strengths, the school must, at a later
stage in the marketing cycle, capitalise on them by:

- seeking ways to communicate these strengths to the internal
  market and the external clients;
- looking for opportunities to apply the successful strategies in
  other areas;
- ensuring that reinforcement and praise are given;
- ensuring that such activities receive continued support —
  should these perceived strengths now appear to the senior
  management team to be activities which need phasing out,
  the change will need very careful handling!

Our experience from running many training days in schools is that
it is not always easy to articulate precisely what the strengths are.
Exercise One (Page 72) provides an example of comparing the views
of staff with the views of different client groups in the internal
market. Very often we have found that they are not all that
fundamentally different but that there is a differing emphasis and
articulation. It is important that these views are integrated in such
a way as to provide a consistent message about the school.

Weaknesses

Again, as the name suggests, these are self-explanatory — the things
which the school or area does badly. A possible problem here is that
staff may be unwilling to articulate problems if they believe that
there is an element of accountability present. Realistic self-
evaluation or team evaluation will be minimal in such circumstances.
Staff will not be honest about themselves and all weaknesses will be

of other areas and activities. They need to feel that there is a sense of trust and that what they say will not be used out of context. It is therefore important to have the right context and climate before starting a SWOT analysis. Often schools may prefer to use the term 'areas for development' so as to avoid the negative or critical application of 'weaknesses'.

Having identified certain weaknesses, it will be necessary to plan to overcome them. This is where the marketing cycle overlaps with the quality control of the educational product. However, it may be that those who identified the weaknesses were only *perceiving* a problem which did not, in fact, exist. For example, parents may feel that there are not enough textbooks in a particular subject area when, in fact, much of the source material is to be found in attractive, up-to-date booklets which are produced by the school. In such cases, communication needs to be improved.

Opportunities

These are potential openings which could be grasped in the future. If the school or area does not identify these as early as possible, it will not be able to plan resources so that the opportunities can be grasped at the appropriate time. Another school could be more farsighted and gain an advantage.

In order to list the opportunities, it is necessary to have a clear view of the environment in which the school will operate in the medium to long term. Nothing is static; the educational world has changed very radically over the last ten years and probably will continue to do so. There is a need to be creative so a broad perspective is required. Outsiders to the school or unit will be helpful in determining the likely opportunities that may be presented in the future. Once the opportunities have been listed, the school can prioritise them for immediate action in the short term or for longer term consideration. In order to prioritise, the school will have to consider which opportunities will be lost if they are not grasped relatively quickly and which ones the school can afford to develop later.

Threats

As with the identification of possible opportunities, there needs to be some degree of vision about the future educational environment if potential threats to the school or area are to be highlighted in plenty of time so that they can be countered. Having identified certain potential threats, it is important to take action to avoid them and, better still, to turn such threats into opportunities. For example, a school threatened with the loss of some of its playing fields for building land could simply campaign against this. More positively, it could build links with community organisations so that the land was seen locally as a community asset and less 'dispensable'.

The possible drawbacks of the SWOT approach can be considered to be that:

- it gathers very subjective views
- it encourages fault-finding
- because of their diversity the results cannot easily be summarised or aggregated
- it is not weighted so that minor and major issues may be given equal prominence.

The advantages of the approach are that:

- it can be applied at the whole school or area level
- it is quick and easy to carry out
- it does not require any special skill or equipment in order to carry it out or to analyse it.

A practical SWOT analysis for a school

Figure 5.2 is an example of a SWOT analysis of a secondary school. It has been compiled by the teaching staff completing part of the form and the parent governors and representatives of the PTA completing the other column. This activity took place when the parental representatives joined the teachers on a training day which dealt with marketing the school.

We shall now comment on some of the categories and compare the responses by the two groups.

(i) Strengths — it is interesting how the different groups prioritise different items. School staff often assume that the academic quality is good but do not emphasise how well the pupils perform in tests and examinations. However, this is often a critical factor for parents. Schools must recognise this parental want, giving it due priority and publicity in order to maximise the perceived strength. The discussion earlier in the book about overt and covert performance indicators is one to bear in mind in these sections. Good examination results are obviously perceived as a strong overt performance indicator by parents whereas in the next section covert factors, such as school uniform, play a part in the perceived weaknesses of the school.

	STAFF PERCEPTIONS	CLIENT PERCEPTIONS
STRENGTHS	well qualified, committed staff caring environment wide range of extra-curricular activities stable staff	good exam results music provision attractive brochure sports facilities stable staff
WEAKNESSES	inconsistent disciplinary procedures state of fabric of building narrow corridors application of equal opportunities policy lack of career development provision for gifted links with governors	uniform rules not strict enough making phone contact in a morning erratic homework pupils not stretched enough classes too large
OPPORTUNITIES	adult learners creche on site industrial and international exchanges letting the premises	widen community links industry links develop more languages
THREATS	difficulty recruiting certain staff high cost of current staff senior management time used on administration neighbouring school's marketing campaign	shortage of specialist staff resource shortages effect of national politics

Figure 5.2   A completed SWOT analysis

(ii) Weaknesses — clients' perceptions of the school's weaknesses can be split into things that can be adjusted easily, like organising better telephone access, and those which need more concerted activity, such as extending the pupils academically. It is also important to note the way in which uniform figures significantly in parental opinion. Similarly, of the weaknesses perceived by the staff, some can obviously be attended to more easily, such as strengthening links with the governors, while some aspects, such as a more coherent career development framework, will take significant management action over a longer time frame.

(iii) Opportunities — seeking the opinion of wider client groups has provided a range of ideas. Amalgamation of the two lists will provide a valuable agenda for investigation and action in order to exploit the school's potential.

(iv) Threats — some of these are national issues and are therefore difficult for an individual school to deal with, for example staff shortages in certain subject areas. However, there are things that the school can do to limit the damage, such as considering making use of the articled teacher scheme or attracting staff by giving help with accommodation. The underfunding of education has led to resource shortages but there is little which a school can do in the short term to improve overall national funding. However, opting out of LEA control may produce significant short term gains for the individual school. Recognition of resource shortages may, however, lead to a consideration of sponsorship as an alternative source of revenue. The final threat on the list, the marketing campaign of the neighbouring school, can be countered and we hope that this book helps in that endeavour.

2. General Questionnaires

Once the school has identified the area of activity about which it wishes to sample the clients and/or professionals, it may be appropriate to design a questionnaire which will elicit the required information. This could be carried out by post, by telephone or through personal interviews. The questionnaire can be a way of working towards a SWOT analysis or it can be a different information gathering activity. The main benefits of this approach are:

- attention can be focused on the particular area of information which the school requires;
- it collects primary information direct from the clients;
- it covers a broad sample of clients so that generalisations and inferences can be drawn.

The drawbacks of using this approach mainly centre on:

- the time needed to draw up and administer the questionnaire and to analyse the data;
- the delay in obtaining the information;
- the expense of the materials and the time needed to obtain the information.

A practical example of the questionnaire approach

Figure 5.3 from the Cambridge Accountability Project samples home/school links and provides a good example of the questionnaire approach. It asks specific questions to particular clients so that the responses can be used to inform the way in which the school develops its parental links in the future.

The questionnaire approach can be seen to be a very specific information sampling device. The approach is one of highlighting a series of key areas of home/school communications: newsletters, reports, information booklets and parents' meetings and assessing clients' views on the strengths and weaknesses of the school's performance in these key areas. This specific targeting of an area can be very useful once a general concern has been identified. It provides the detailed information which will be required by management in order to assess the area in depth and to produce recommendations for improvement. The direct value of the approach is based on clients' experiences and views of what the school is offering.

3 Professional evaluation instruments

As the title suggests these are the approaches which are used by professionals in the school in order to assess what the school currently has to offer in terms of its product and service. It is possible to choose from a variety of techniques such as Guidelines for Review and Internal Development in Schools (GRIDS) and Diagnosis of Individual and Organisational Need (DION) for evaluating the school's activities. Some of these (such as DION) can be carried out and analysed quite quickly but others involve a gradual process of determining problems and identifying priority areas for improvement. Evaluations carried out by other professionals such as HMI and LEA Inspectors can also provide significant instruments for evaluation and improvement. Any of these instruments can form part of the normal process of evaluating a school's activities but they are also valuable in that they provide information to feed into the marketing process. Schools must develop an understanding of the concept of quality and a means of monitoring this if they are to

Questionnaire sent to parents in the Holbein case study (Cambridge Accountability Project, 1981, vol. 3, pp. 79 – 80).

CAMBRIDGE ACCOUNTABILITY PROJECT

Parents' views

The questions below ask for your views about certain information given to you by Holbein School (e.g. in Newsletters, Reports, booklets, etc.).

Your replies will be treated in the strictest confidence. There is no need to give your name.

Each question asks you to tick the box which most closely represents your view. If you wish to give more information, please write on the back of the form or on a separate sheet. All your views will be of great interest to the Project.

Could you return the form in the stamped addressed envelope provided, to Dr Rex Gibson, Cambridge Institute of Education, Shaftesbury Road, Cambridge, CB2 2BX.

TICK ONE BOX FOR EACH QUESTION

1.   NEWSLETTERS: Every year the school sends out a number of Newsletters to parents

   a) Do the Newsletters contain:

Too much information?	Too little information?	About the right amount?
☐	☐	☐

   b) Would you prefer:

More Newsletters?	Fewer Newsletters?	About the same number?
☐	☐	☐

2.   REPORTS: Every year the school sends out a Report to parents on their child's progress.

   (You may not yet have received all the reports. Please answer for those reports you have received.)

   a) Do you think the Reports give:

	Too much information?	Too little information?	About the right amount?
Third Year Reports	☐	☐	☐
Fourth Year Reports	☐	☐	☐
Fifth Year Reports	☐	☐	☐

   b) In your experience, are the Reports generally written:

In too technical (or too difficult) language?	In a way that is usually easy to understand?
☐	☐

Figure 5.3   Cambridge accountability project

3. INFORMATION BOOKLETS: The School issues a number of booklets giving detailed
   information about Holbein. You may not yet have received all these booklets but
   could you answer the questions for those booklets of which you do have knowledge.

   a) INFORMATION FOR NEW STUDENTS AND THEIR PARENTS (A booklet for New parents and students)

   (i) Did this give:

Too much information?	Too little information?	About the right amount?
☐	☐	☐

   (ii) Did you find it:

Written in too technical (or difficult) language?	At about the right level for understanding?
☐	☐

   b) FOURTH YEAR CHOICES?   (A booklet about the Fourth Year to enable students to choose options)

   (i) Did this give:

Too much information?	Too little information?	About the right amount?
☐	☐	☐

   (ii) Did you find it:

Written in too technical (or difficult) language?	At about the right level for understanding?
☐	☐

   c) THE SIXTH YEAR (A booklet about the Sixth Form)

   (i) Did this give:

Too much information?	Too little information?	About the right amount?
☐	☐	☐

   (ii) Did you find it:

Written in too technical (or difficult)language?	At about the right level for understanding?
☐	☐

4. PARENTS MEETINGS: The School arranges parents' evenings to discuss Reports and students'
    progress

    a) Would you prefer   More   Fewer   The
                                 parents' evenings? parents' evenings? present number?

                                 ☐   ☐   ☐

    b) How would you describe   Generally   Generally
       your feelings about   satisfied   dissatisfied
       what happens at the
       Parents' evenings   ☐   ☐
       you have attended?

5. If you had a problem about your son's/daughter's schooling, or if you just wished to
    find out something further about Holbein School:

    a) Do you think it   Easy to make contact   Difficult to make contact
       would be: with the school?   with the school?

                                  ☐   ☐

    b) Would you yourself: Feel hesitant (or   Not feel hesitant (or
                                  unsure) about contact-   unsure) about contacting
                                  ing the School?   the school?

                                  ☐   ☐

6. How much do you feel you   I feel I know a good   I feel I know   I feel I know
    know about what happens   deal about   a moderate   very little
    at Holbein School?   the School   amount   about the School
    (Tick the box which best
     describes your feeling)   ☐   ☐   ☐

7. Do you think that as a   I feel I should have   I think I already
    parent you should have   more say in what   have sufficient
    more say in what goes on   goes on at the School   say in what goes on
    at the School?
                                  ☐   ☐
    (Tick the box that best
     describes your feeling)

8. Would you recommend   Yes   Perhaps   No
    Holbein School to
    your friends?   ☐   ☐   ☐

    (Tick the box that best
     describes your feeling)

Thank you for answering the questions. If there is any further information you would
like to give, please write in the space overleaf or on a separate sheet. Any of your
views will be very welcome and will be treated in the strictest confidence.

Please return this sheet in the attached envelope provided to: Dr D. R. Gibson,
Cambridge Institute of Education, Shaftesbury Road, Cambridge, CB2 2BX.

continue to supply a product and service which meets the clients' expectations. This concept of quality control will be considered in Chapter Nine.

Conclusion

Chapter Four dealt with the educational context and what the market wants and needs from the school. This chapter has assessed approaches which analyse where the school is now and what it has to offer. We do not pretend that this is an easy process; it is confused by the fact that there are no Platonic 'absolute values' but, very often, highly subjective perceptions of what the school currently provides. By combining the views of staff, parents, pupils and other clients using the various exercises at the end of this chapter a pattern can be built up of the strengths and weaknesses of the school. This will help to analyse its current position. Such an approach which assesses the perceptions of the school can be combined with internal evaluation approaches used by professionals. It is only then, when a clear picture of what the school is offering or, more significantly, is perceived as offering, that this evidence can be analysed in the context of what the market wants and a reconciliation attempted. This reconciliation, ie the definition of the product and service to be offered, forms the basis of Chapter Six.

Chapter five: exercise one

---

*STAFF ANALYSIS OF STRENGTHS AND
WEAKNESSES*

Self-managing schools under an LMS or GMS framework
have considerable autonomy to manage their own affairs.
One key element in the success of this is how well the school
relates to its local community and communicates the
positive things that it does. In this context fill in the list
below:

A. As teachers give three or four strengths and
    weaknesses of your school

    Write down three or four strengths and weaknesses
    of your school as perceived by parents

    Are the strengths and weaknesses perceived
    differently by the pupils in your school? — Give
    examples.

B. Would you send your child to this school — if so,
    why? If not, why not?

    Would you recommend a colleague to work at your
    school?

Chapter five: exercise two

STRENGTHS AND WEAKNESSES OF AN AREA OF THE SCHOOL

A. As teachers give three or four strengths and weaknesses of your Department/Year group

B. Write down three or four strengths and weaknesses of your Department/Year group as perceived by other colleagues in your school

C. Write down three or four strengths and weaknesses of your Department/Year group as perceived by parents (using information gained through market research)

D. Are the strengths and weaknesses perceived differently by the pupils in your school? — give examples

Chapter five: exercise three

GENERAL QUESTIONNAIRE APPROACHES

Adapt the questionnaire on pages 68 to 70 in order to gather information about a specific aspect of your school.

6 Defining and redefining a school's product and service

It is no longer safe to assume a secure, captive market for a school's product and service. This is because of demographic changes, open enrolment legislation and increasing parental awareness of the subsequent element of choice. If the school is to be an outward looking organisation, its efforts should be focused on the wants and needs of its client groups. This contrasts with prevalent attitudes in some schools where, traditionally, staff have put their interests as producers of education first. The new market environment has often been represented as a considerable shift in emphasis from 'producer capture' towards 'consumer power'. In the context of this changed and more competitive educational market an individual school must clarify and define what it is trying to achieve and then communicate this effectively to the internal and external markets. There is a consequent need to reformulate whole school aims and objectives and then, if necessary, to adjust or develop some of the school's activities.

The critical activity before the marketing strategy can be developed is to determine the educational product and service which the school will offer. This strategic management activity is carried out by assessing the significance of the information from market research (Chapter Four) and the analysis of the school's product (Chapter Five) and then reconciling the two. This can be expressed in Figure 6.1.

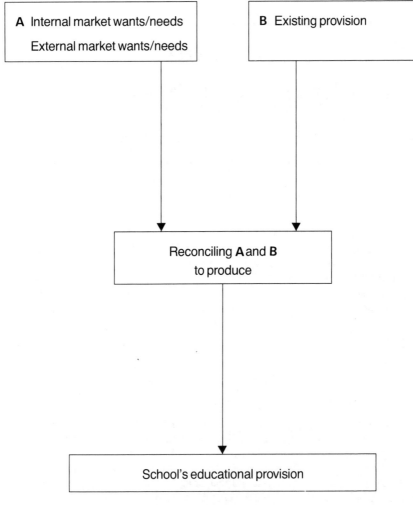

Figure 6.1 Determining the educational product and service

Definition process

This section will now consider how this strategic process works. The process of defining a school's educational provision can be seen as going through four stages:

1. *Vision*

The first stage of the four stage process, that of establishing a vision, is achieved by combining the leader's educational values and sense of purpose with the interpretation of the information gathered through research (A & B in the diagram on page 76) in a broad strategic way. The school can then have a clear sense of its direction and purpose over the next five years and can communicate these to the internal and external market.

There is considerable evidence to support the view that one of the most significant factors in a school's success is the quality of its leadership. One of the key roles of a leader is to develop a vision of where the organisation is going. Such a vision should be set within the context of the educational market environment and should provide challenging and inspiring goals as well as being desirable and humanly achievable. The vision looks into the future so it is, by its very nature, a strategic view. It will be broadbased so as to be fairly stable over time with inbuilt flexibility in execution. To be effective, the vision of what the school seeks to be must be communicated and make sense to others, both in the organisation and outside. It is not just a pious statement of intent. The leader must be committed to achieving the vision through the planned aims and activities of the school. For example, the vision might include the desire to be a school which serves the whole range of ability and to link into the wider community as much as possible.

2. *Mission*

A very good definition of 'mission' is provided by Bennis and Nanus (1985):

> 'The primary use of a mission is to gain the attention of people at all levels of the organisation, to focus their activities on a common broad purpose. Out of mission come objectives which crystallise the generalisation of the vision into tangible, realisable, but still very broad goals.'

If the vision for the school is to be articulated in a form that is to be understood by others, then a written statement of purpose or a mission statement must be provided. This should encapsulate the goals of the school, crystallising its purposes and values. This is not a pious statement like a school motto in Latin *'In Deificatis Educatoribus Scientiae credimus'* ('In the DES we trust') or 'Nisi DES frustra' ('Nothing is possible without the DES') but a practical summary of the key goals of the school. It defines the boundaries of the school's activities and beliefs providing a focus and purpose for the individuals who work in the school. As it is a positive statement defining the purpose of the school, it will also tell the reader what the school will not do or accept. The significance of the mission statement is that the school does not need a series of negative statements, encapsulated in a set of school rules stating a number of 'don'ts'. If the mission statement puts forward that the school is a caring school then, by definition, it does not allow stealing, bullying or fighting! People at all levels of the organisation can then focus their activities on a common broad purpose and jointly supported values. An example of a mission statement could be:

> Brentwich School fosters academic and personal development in a caring and challenging environment so that each individual can achieve his or her full potential.

What does this statement tell us? The following interpretation can be made by examining the key words:

- academic — traditional learning values and achievements;
- personal development — educating the whole person;
- caring environment — looking after people, respect for others and their property, acceptable standards of behaviour that display 'care for others';
- challenging environment — encouraging and expecting individuals to strive for improvement and excellence;
- each individual — members of the school community are treated as individuals rather than in a general way;
- achieve full potential — delivering the most important performance indicator.

Thus the mission statement provides a simple framework from which further, more detailed aims and objectives can be derived.

To ensure that this common, broad purpose exists in reality, the *process* of creating the mission statement is as important as the statement itself. If it is to represent shared goals and if these are to be realised through the school's activities, then a shared process of developing the statement will be necessary. This will allow for an exchange of views, an understanding of the perceptions of others and the development of a common statement with which the partners feel a sense of ownership. Above all, there should then be a sense of commitment to the statement. This process of discussing and deciding cannot be overemphasised as the important method by which a school builds its own sense of purpose and achieves staff commitment to it. Research on what makes a 'good' school consistently reports that effective schools have high levels of shared and understood goals that have been developed by the involvement and commitment of staff working as a team. Although such a process sounds simple enough to put into effect, there may be problems because of different perceptions about the school's purposes and values between the different stakeholders and even between the teachers themselves.

The question therefore arises concerning who should be involved in developing this mission statement. It is essential to involve the governors and staff (including non-teaching staff). Some schools may wish to consult more widely but, in order to manage time effectively, it could be legitimate to consider that wider groups such as parents, local industry and the local community are already represented through the Governing Body.

The statement itself should be clear and concise (about twenty five words) and should express the values, purposes and intentions of the school. Each component phrase should be carefully considered because each should be achievable rather than just a pious hope. All members of the group involved in drawing up the statement should give careful thought to the identification of the values, beliefs, ambitions, intentions and purposes of the school and then, either individually or in small groups should develop key words to encapsulate these. These would then be shared in a larger group in order to remove synonymous expressions and to achieve commonality. From this refined list of key words a statement can be constructed. This would be agreed and communicated to all the school's partners at the appropriate time.

The importance of the mission statement should not be underestimated. It serves as the cornerstone of the school's purpose and function as well as being central to the marketing strategy. It should be used in several ways:

- to inform the development of the school's aims and hence the products and services needed to achieve the mission;
- to act as a statement against which the potential of new initiatives can first be checked. For example if the mission statement incorporates reference to equality of opportunity

for all, it would be inappropriate to introduce any form of grouping that disadvantaged individual pupils. Such a major change would involve reconsideration of the school's mission before implementation;

- to help to focus the marketing process by giving a clear view of what the organisation is trying to do;
- to enable any 'ambassador' to explain clearly what the school is trying to achieve and to ensure that the various ambassadors put out the same message.

Stakeholders (governors, staff, pupils and parents) thus get a clear understanding of what the school does and what it wants to do in serving client needs.

3. *Aims*

Both the mission statement and the whole school aims which are developed from it 'belong' to the organisation. Aims set out the broad path to be followed by the school as it attempts to meet the wants and needs of the clients. An aim is created by taking a key word from the mission statement and turning it into statements of intent. The school can then focus on these statements when deciding the objectives and activities which are needed in order to realise the vision and the mission of the school.

As with the mission statement, it is important that there is a sense of ownership of the aims in order to increase the chance of them being achieved. A school must decide how best to review and redefine its aims. In most schools the teaching staff already participate fully in this process but the governors and senior management might consider broadening the process to include non-teaching staff and the parents who, after all, are the clients. While there are problems of getting agreement between the parties it is important to discuss, to have a common view and to reach a consensus.

The frequency with which aims are redefined will be partly determined by the rate of change in the educational environment. It is generally accepted that they should be reviewed (even if this does not result in alteration) every four years. Because they are broad-based they do not change frequently, even if the staff or parents change.

Educational institutions are largely staffed by professionals, so there has, in the past, been a tendency to allow individuals a lot of freedom to use their professional judgement in deciding how best to achieve the aims of the organisation. Indeed, these aims may not always have been stated clearly. This has led to a situation in which individuals have either tended to pursue their own goals (deliberately) or have misinterpreted (genuinely) the aims of the school. The result may have been a conflicting message for pupils and thus confusion for these and other clients. This lack of common purpose would cause considerable frustration and pupils' activities would lack direction. If a school is to be effective, the staff should all be working to achieve an agreed set of aims.

4.   *Objectives*

Where previously we have been considering the broad concepts of vision and purpose, when it comes to objectives the emphasis shifts to quantifiable and measurable activities. Objectives are often set in a short to medium term context (up to three years) as an operational or tactical planning device. Thus once the school aims have been stated in general terms, corporate or whole school objectives will be developed and will relate to the achievement of these aims (and thus to the mission statement). They will be redefined more frequently than aims, usually at annual intervals. If purposeful, goal-directed activity is to take place, the setting of specific objectives will be necessary for all the school's activities eg for the curriculum, pastoral care, staff development and marketing.

These objectives will:

- provide a coherent approach across the different areas of the school;
- define narrower targets in order to achieve the school's mission and aims;
- quantify those targets which the school can realistically achieve.

Objectives are, therefore, a way of specifying what needs to be done across the areas of the school within a given time. If objectives are understood by all staff in a school they will help to form a framework on which the activities of the school can be based. When planning objectives there are various management points to bear in mind and these will be outlined in the ensuing paragraphs. Most significantly, objectives should be quantifiable and expressed in concrete terms. It is important that these specific objectives are set in relation to the strategic perspective identified in the long-term planning process.

While aims are fairly broad, objectives need to be quite *specific*. Each should be a clear, concise statement of what is to be achieved. They should be *written* and communicated so that everyone is aware of what they are. They can then be referred to and used as a tool to facilitate such activities as decision-making, monitoring and evaluation. The *relevance* of the objective should be checked. They should be appropriate to the stated aims of the school, rather than to an individual or sub-group's desire to maximise their own aims. *Agreement* with the objectives will help to ensure that they are seen to be important and that activity will be directed towards their achievement. It is particularly because of their potential for evaluating activities that objectives should be *measurable*. If some form of quantitative criteria can be established then the evaluation process can be carried out objectively and efficiently.

It is generally accepted that people are motivated by success and that it is often easier to work towards realistic short-term targets. This principle can be applied to the setting of objectives. All those concerned need to believe that the targets are being set at a level which is *achievable*. If not, there will be disenchantment because those who have framed the objectives will be perceived to be 'out of touch' with reality in the organisation. There must be a belief that, through purposeful activity, the objectives can be achieved. However, objectives should not be set which, at the outset, are demonstrably too easy to achieve. If schools are fully to develop their pupils, then *challenging* activities need to be provided. Similarly, challenging objectives should motivate staff and encourage creativity.

The *timescales* over which different objectives should be achieved may vary considerably, depending on the level at which they are applied. Nevertheless, a time by which they must be achieved should be stated. If not, those involved will be unclear about what is expected and monitoring and control will be ineffective.

To summarise, and to use an acronym which will be familiar to some readers, objectives should be challenging and:

S	pecific
M	easurable
A	greed and Achievable
R	elevant
T	imed

Example of the process

The following sequence of activities was introduced at the beginning of this chapter. It involves a process of developing shared visions

VISION   of a caring school which is outward looking
                        and intellectually stretches children of all
                        abilities.

MISSION   *Brentwich School fosters academic and
                        personal development in a caring and
                        challenging environment so that each
                        individual can achieve his or her full potential.*

AIMS   1. *To provide stimulating and challenging
                            teaching materials.*

                        2. To provide extension and support materials for
                            different ability levels.

                        3. To develop high expectation levels of individual
                            performance.

                        4. To set targets for each group and individual.

OBJECTIVES   1. To investigate the type of materials which fulfil
                            Aim 1 above.

                        2. To provide time and support for staff to
                            examine approaches and materials available
                            and to adapt them if necessary.

                        3. To evaluate the use of such materials in
                            increasing pupil involvement and learning.

Figure 6.2 Translating the vision into practice

into activities so that the product and service matches the clients' wants and needs. An example of the way in which this can work in practice is demonstrated in Figure 6.2 where a mission statement has been developed from a broad vision for the school. One aspect of the mission statement (challenging environment) is taken and, from this, a series of four aims are developed. One of these aims (to provide stimulating and challenging teaching materials) is then translated into objectives through which it can be realised.

By going through this process, clear objectives can be developed which relate to the achievement of the school's mission. It is then necessary to attach timescales to the objectives in order to assist in the planning process. These objectives will be used to determine the activities required and to measure performance at a later stage. If all the partners have a clear view of what needs doing and if this relates to client wants and needs, then the school will demonstrate quality in its management thinking and in educational outcomes.

Conclusion

When the school has used this process to develop a coherent product and service, it is important, first of all, to communicate this to the *internal* market. Only when there is a clear internal view of the school's product and service can the focus on the *external* marketing strategy begin. The possible nature of the promotional activities and the way in which the marketing strategy can be managed will be considered in Chapters Seven and Eight.

Reference

Bennis W. and Nanus A., *Leaders: the strategies of taking charge.* Harper & Row (1985)

Chapter six: exercise one

PREPARING A MISSION STATEMENT

A mission statement summarises the main purposes of the school in no more than 25 words. Ideally this is a group activity for all the staff.

A. Write down the key words which encapsulate the values and purposes of the school.

Share these and decide on the most significant and commonly agreed.

B. Prepare individually a mission statement for a school.

Agree within the group a common mission statement.

Chapter six: exercise two

MISSION INTO REALITY

Having completed Exercise One translate the mission statement into a series of aims and objectives following the
pattern demonstrated in this chapter.

7 Promotional approaches and techniques

Before deciding on the marketing strategy which will be used to promote the school's product and service, there has to be a review of the variety of promotional approaches and techniques that are appropriate to secondary schools and of the management issues surrounding each one of them. No simple categorisation of promotional approaches is possible but, for ease of reference, this chapter divides them into seven main types which are:

- Prospectuses, brochures and flyers
- Other written material
- The media
- Advertising
- Word of mouth
- Other communication techniques
- Group promotion.

However, before examining each approach in turn, we must remind the reader of the existence of the internal as well as the external markets.

Those who constitute the internal market, such as staff, existing pupils and their parents, are the ambassadors of the school in the wider community, ie in the external market. When considering promotional approaches, the school's first priority must be to ensure that these ambassadors have accurate and positive information to disseminate. Management should be confident that there is a consistent message going out about the aims of the school and about the activities which are taking place in order to achieve those aims. This information may be in a visual form such as a prospectus, brochure, other publication or pieces of pupils' work but it is equally likely to be delivered by word of mouth. Therefore who delivers the information, and how it is delivered can give hidden messages because of the way the information is transmitted. It is very important that there is an awareness of the significance of the delivery method as well as the message which is being delivered. We will now deal with each promotional approach in turn.

1   Prospectuses, brochures and flyers

Although many people use the terms interchangeably, there is a difference between a prospectus and a brochure. While a prospectus is obviously designed to be an attractive promotional document it must also comply with the statutory requirements for prospectuses in maintained schools. A school *must* have a prospectus but decisions can then be made about whether to have other material for either promotion or information. An example of such material would be a brochure which can be a much shorter document designed to encourage prospective parents to contact the school. Similarly, flyers which are flat or folded single sheets of information, can attract potential clients to the school in a very cost effective way. Each of these documents is described in more detail below and the characteristics of good document design which can be applied by the reader are also outlined.

(i)   Prospectus

First impressions are important so that a lot of schools are developing high quality glossy prospectuses. Such publications are designed to impress so they focus on the strong points of the schools such as the extensive playing fields, the well equipped laboratories and the attentive pupils. There is usually reference to a caring community and the development of the full potential of every pupil. There can be hidden messages conveyed through visual images, for example the ex-grammar school which reminds clients of its 'traditional' values by giving prominence to the school crest and motto. Public schools have long practised the art of summing up a great many messages in one photograph. Two pupils, a boy and girl in traditional uniform, textbooks under the arm, standing in front of the school chapel would represent the school as follows:

- uniform = standards and discipline
- textbooks = academic standards and study
- the chapel = traditional values and approaches
- a boy and girl = a mixed school.

All these messages can be conveyed in one photograph. If the prospectus is to attract clients, the text and graphics should reflect the wants of the clients in that particular school's community (as identified through market research).

It is important to achieve a balance between the quality of presentation and the information being transmitted. If the document is too glossy and superficial some parents may ask what is missing or being covered up? It may, under a delegated budgetary system, raise questions about money being better spent on pupils and not being wasted! However, the counter argument is that, because of formula funding, if the prospectus brings in an extra ten pupils (yielding £15,000) and costs the school £2000, then it could be considered worthwhile and cost effective.

As was mentioned earlier there is a legal obligation for all maintained schools to have a prospectus. This acts as a parents' handbook in that it must set out basic information about the school such as the name of the head and chair of governors, the charging policy and the uniform requirements. The complete requirements for a school prospectus are as follows:

- Name, address and telephone number of school and its classification (type)
- Name of headteacher and chair of governors
- Affiliation with any religious denomination and particulars of religious education
- The aims of the school
- The governors' statement of curricular aims
- The school curriculum, its content and organisation for each year group (including groupings of children, cross-curricular themes and subject choices and levels)
- Provision for students with special needs
- Homework arrangements
- Pastoral care arrangements
- Sex education
- Careers education
- Examination entry policy
- Public examination results, in a specified form
- Time of school sessions, dates of school terms and holidays
- Provision for collective worship and withdrawal arrangements
- Out of school activities
- Uniform requirements, PE kit
- Charging policy
- Discipline arrangements and school rules
- How parents can visit the school or make a complaint

D

- Availability of certain specified information
- Transfer arrangements to next school
- Arrangements for prospective parents to visit.

It is important for the school to ensure that the information in the prospectus is accurate despite the fact that it may change quite frequently. There are various ways of achieving this accuracy. One is to regularly reprint and recirculate a highly professional, glossy publication that covers the legal requirements but refers parents to more detailed documentation in the school which amplifies the basic information provided. A second option is to produce a high quality folder with similarly high quality sheets which fit inside it. While a long print run may be used for the folder the inserts can be changed each year. This avoids some of the obvious drawbacks of the high cost related to the possibly quite minor amendments about which the parents have to be informed. A third option is to produce a cheaper publication on the school premises using in-house desktop publishing facilities. This can produce reasonable quality at a lower price than using a commercial typesetter and printer.

Additionally the school can produce information sheets for other purposes. These will provide details which either:

1. change frequently, eg staff lists

or

2. only apply to certain groups, eg option details

Although they are not an integral part of the prospectus or brochure it is important that each sheet is properly presented. Tenth generation photocopies will do nothing to enhance a school's reputation. The advantage of this approach is that the sheets can be used separately for their specific purpose or combined together to form the last section of the prospectus.

Key points in prospectus design   There are many management considerations which the school has to bear in mind when undertaking the production of a prospectus. A number of specific points are listed below against which schools can check their own prospectus:

1. *Decide on the purpose — is it for marketing, for reference or both?* Is the prospectus going to include everything or is more detail going to be found in the school. Is it to be a handbook which acts as a complete reference document or is it to be a focused document that is the central point in

projecting the right image for the school? There is the
danger of trying to do too many things in the prospectus so
that it becomes cluttered and loses its impact.

2. *There should be a simple, eye catching and tasteful cover.* It is
especially important to try out prospective designs on
clients to get their opinion on what is effective.

3. *Decide on the key issues in the prospectus.* State the school's
mission near the beginning and then reinforce key words
from the mission statement in the various sections. In order
to get across a sense of purpose and a clear message, readers
need to know straight away what the school stands for.
Therefore it is very important that the mission statement is
at the beginning. Bad prospectus design results in the
reader having to turn four or five pages to find this information.

4. *Decide on the strengths to put across.* This can be done either
explicitly through describing them in the written text or
implicitly, eg through the inclusion of key photographs. The
right photograph can be worth a thousand words; in the
case mentioned earlier from a public school, the picture in
front of the chapel provides an example of this. Similarly,
messages are conveyed by lists such as those which contain
staff qualifications.

5. *Structure it clearly.* Bold headings and concise text broken up
by appropriate photographs or charts would obviously be
better than columns of dense text.

6. *Have the reader in mind.* The danger of teachers preparing
a prospectus is that they may use language and jargon that
is common to them but not so clearly understood by the
wider community. It is important to realise that several different types of audience displaying different levels of
understanding of the education world will read the document. It must be written in clear straightforward language
which will be easily understood by these different readers.
This is not an easy task but one that is critical to the success
of the document. A group of parents and pupils can assist
here.

7. *Make it easy to read.* Following on from the point above, it
is worth comparing an income tax form and an application
form for a competition in a tabloid newspaper. The former
will be far less comprehensible. The authors do not
necessarily advocate adopting the latter's style but it does
make the point. Thus, those producing the material should
focus on four factors: the length of the sentences or
paragraphs, the reading age and educational knowledge of

the reader, the use of appropriate language and the use of both attractive and suitable type sizes. There should be a friendly welcoming style which leaves the reader wanting to know more.

8. *Use high quality illustrations.* Whether they are photographs or line drawings they are not just there to fill up space but to make the document visually exciting and interesting, to convey messages and, above all, to keep the clients reading and looking!

9. *Do not make the prospectus too long.* As well as adding to the expense, effectiveness is often lost after the first few pages. There is a need to establish ideas and information in a precise and concise way and not to have the reader over-come with the volume. National Curriculum documentation should not provide the exemplar!

10. *Do not normally include material which dates.* For most schools it is too costly to reset the prospectus completely each year. Such information can be provided as an insert or loose sheets inside the back cover.

11. *Ensure that there is a prominent display of how to contact the school.* We have come across several prospectuses with blank back covers! While this is an obvious waste of space it also wastes the most important use of the back page. This is for a map of where to find the school, its address and telephone number and who to contact. Thus the most important information concerning how to follow up the initial interest aroused by the prospectus comes at the appropriate place and is prominently displayed if the prospectus is left on a table.

12. *Ensure that the prospectus has a professional appearance.* We have traditionally undersold education. If schools believe that they deliver quality in educational terms, then they should represent that quality in other activities. Some schools deliberately go in for marketing acts of self deprecation by producing poorly printed information. The business that has a £1m to £3m income should not represent itself as an amateurish enterprise because it does not take itself or, more importantly, its clients seriously and so produces second class materials.

There is no identikit perfect prospectus or structure that we could recommend, nor would we want to do so. Each school must use an approach which best suits its individual needs and which appeals to the clients in the area. We suggest that, in evaluating prospectuses, readers ensure that the statutory information is included and that the points listed above are applied. One example of 'good practice' which we have come across locally is the prospectus of Granby High School in Harrogate. It is reproduced in Figure 7.1 not as an ideal which would necessarily be suitable for transfer to other schools, but to show how, by careful consideration of legal requirements and our design criteria, a first class product can be created.

Exercise:
The reader can now reflect on the extent to which the legal requirements and the key points on pages 89 to 92 have been applied by those who designed the Granby High School prospectus.

It must be pointed out that this is a high quality colour prospectus which has been printed professionally and it cannot be done justice when replicated and reduced in black and white to suit the requirement of this book. Nevertheless, we still think it provides a suitable exemplar of good practice.

(ii) Brochures

Rather than being a totally different publication in terms of content, the brochure can be a shortened version of the prospectus. It is used for publicity purposes where more general information is needed for a wider audience. In fact, because of resource constraints, most schools rely on the use of a comprehensive prospectus or a limited flyer as promotional literature.

(iii) Flyers

These are usually double sided folded sheets of A3 or A4 paper. They act as introductory leaflets or tasters and are used to cover a wider geographical area than the prospectus or brochure. Very often a flyer can be of immense value if it gives the name and type of school and some basic information including a map of the school's location and who to contact. They are obviously relatively cheap to produce and can be taken to local estate agents, removal firms etc for distribution with their normal literature. This will create an awareness of where the school is and what it does so that those whose interest is aroused can telephone the school for the full prospectus. Some schools not only put the name of the headteacher and the school telephone number but also two or three current parents (such as members of the PTA) who are prepared to speak to prospective

Figure 7.1   School prospectus

WELCOME

Harrogate Granby High School
Avondale Road
Harrogate
HG1 4AR

Telephone: (0423) 564421

Harrogate Granby High School is a North Yorkshire
County Council 11-18 co-educational, comprehensive
school providing extensive community facilities.

Headteacher: Jonathan Edwards
Chairman of Governors: Dr. Lyle Isaacs.
Vice Chairman of Governors:
Mrs. Margaret-Ann de Courcey-Bayley

The information in this prospectus is designed to reflect
something of the attitudes and values of our school. It will
not answer all your questions; we would prefer to do that
by you visiting us to see the school at work. However, we
do hope that what is included is helpful to both parents
and students and will encourage you to find out more
about us.

Our school community is hard working and friendly.
Achievements and relationships are important to us. All
our students are encouraged to develop their talents to the
full and our academic successes, together with our
growing reputation within the community, illustrate this.
In a well structured environment, where the traditional
values of courtesy and co-operation, enterprise and
initiative are emphasised, learning is enjoyable and
stimulating. We seek to develop a close partnership
between teachers, students, parents and governors. In this
way — together — we can pursue the highest educational
standards for the 1990's.

Such standards become attainable through the
commitment of a highly qualified and well motivated
teaching staff, who work in a well resourced school and in
an attractive working environment. Our School Governors
are active in the life of the school and share with the
teaching staff the following educational aims:

to offer a broad and balanced
curriculum which introduces students
to a wide range of areas of
experience, knowledge and skill;

to help students through hard work,
commitment and self-discipline, to
achieve their potential;

to promote the spiritual, moral,
cultural and physical development of
all students;

to prepare students for the
opportunities, responsibilities and
experiences of adult life in the 1990's
and beyond;

to help students to develop lively,
enquiring and creative minds;

to help students to develop an
awareness of the needs of others.

I hope that you find this prospectus interesting and
informative. To find out more about Harrogate Granby
High School, do not hesitate to contact us. We look
forward to welcoming your child into our school.

Jonathan Edwards
Headteacher

". . . achievements and relationships are important . . ."

Lower School Assembly

Teaching Groups

First Year students (Year 7) spend
some time in mixed ability teaching
groups whilst they settle into the
school and teachers establish their
standards of work and capabilities.
Later, to help them progress at the
appropriate pace, they may be placed
in sets according to their ability. The
size of each teaching group may vary
but from Year 7 to Year 11 seldom
exceeds the mid-twenties; in the Sixth
Form class sizes are close to an
average of twelve.

Lower School students in the Information
Technology Centre

Healthy eating in the Lower School Dining Hall

1

". . . developing talents to the full . . ."

The Curriculum

Our educational aims are put into practice through the
school curriculum; this includes both the programme of
formal timetabled study and all the extra activities which
we provide for our students throughout the school year.
The timetabled lessons include all the subjects described
in the new National Curriculum as well as assemblies and
tutorials which encourage broad and balanced personal
development. In addition, we provide many other
educational experiences and opportunities beyond formal
study; these take place voluntarily at lunchtimes, after
school, at weekends and in an established pattern of
Activities which occupy three consecutive days at the end
of each summer term.

We are proud of the quality of our curriculum and review
it thoroughly each year; what follows in this prospectus
can only represent an outline of it.

A work experience placement at Richard J Eves Associates (Architects)

Specialist equipment for special needs

Lower School PE lesson

'A' Level Physics practical lesson

". . . lively, enquiring and creative minds . . ."

Lower School (Years 7, 8 and 9)

All the subjects of the National Curriculum are taught to all students in these first three years. Additionally, some students study a second European language in Year 8 and in Year 9. In line with the national legislation, we began the new Programmes of Study as required: Mathematics and Science in September 1989 and English and Technology in September 1990. Currently, History and Geography are well prepared for their own timed entry in September 1991. The final group of subjects to join the National Curriculum, (Art, Music, P.E. and Modern Languages) are planning for entry in September 1992.

Upper School (Years 10 and 11)

Our annual process of reviewing what we teach has meant that we are well prepared for the introduction of the new curriculum for this age group in 1992. Currently in Upper School we are able to retain some element of choice for our students, although this will have to decrease slightly in line with the legislation over the next two years. The fundamental choice we ask parents and students to consider is whether to follow a course that leads to G.C.S.E. accreditation in all subjects, or a Pre-vocational Course which allows students to combine essential G.C.S.E. courses with City and Guilds certification and extra work experience.

Sixth Form

Harrogate Granby High School has a large and thriving Sixth Form of nearly 170 full-time students, joined by a small number of adults who attend classes on a part-time basis. The Sixth Form Centre is also the base for numerous courses and recreational activities for the people of Harrogate through our growing Community Programme. The Centre is a hub of activity and a stimulating and challenging environment for young adults preparing to enter the world of employment and higher education. The great majority of our students study at least three or four G.C.E. 'A' Levels but we also offer G.C.S.E. and vocational courses as well as programmes of recreation, of careers and tutorial guidance and of General Studies to complement each student's specialised programme of study.

An 'A' Level History class.

An introduction to the Construction Industry — a careers event for our sixth form students organised by local industry. (Walter G Birch Ltd).

". . . a broad and balanced curriculum . . ."

Curriculum Content

The tables below show the timetabled subjects studied by each year group. Detailed schemes of work for each subject department and the methods of assessment used for each year group are available in the school on request. We hope that parents will discuss both the content of the curriculum that is on offer and how we teach it to their children. We believe that it is the combination of these two elements that produce the quality of the learning experience for our students.

Some of the important themes and issues we teach do not fall neatly into single subject areas: they are of wider concern and affect all of us. We teach these "cross curricular" matters to all our students under the following broad headings:

Economic and Industrial Understanding
Health Education (including aspects of Sex Education)
Citizenship
Environmental Education
Careers Education

Over the last five years, the use of computers by children in schools has developed rapidly. All our departments are well resourced in this area and we are able to provide, in addition, four specialist information technology laboratories, each one equipped with a full range of terminals and accessories to accommodate full teaching groups. We believe that all students must possess computer literacy and have invested successfully to achieve this over recent years.

LOWER SCHOOL
(Years 7, 8 and 9)

UPPER SCHOOL
(Years 10 and 11)

SIXTH FORM

G.C.S.E.

PRE-VOCATIONAL STUDIES

LOWER SCHOOL

UPPER SCHOOL

SIXTH FORM

SUBJECTS TAKEN BY ALL STUDENTS
Mathematics
Science
English
Design Technology
History
Geography
Art
Music
P.E. & Swimming
French or German
R.E.
Modular Studies
Tutorial

SUBJECTS TAKEN BY ALL STUDENTS
Mathematics
Science
English
French or German
PE
Tutorial
Modular Studies

STUDENTS CHOOSE FROM EACH SECTION
A Design Technology subject - C.D.T. or Design or Food Studies or Music Business Studies
A Humanities subject - Geography or History or Religious Studies
and two of the following:
Art and Design
Business Studies
Computer Studies
French
Geography
German
History

SUBJECTS TAKEN BY ALL STUDENTS
Numeracy
Communications
Science
A Foundation Programme
A Design Subject
Information Technology
PE
Tutorial
Modular Studies

STUDENTS CHOOSE OPTIONS
Foreign Language
Engineering
Catering
DIY
Independent Living
Art and Design

SUBJECTS TAKEN BY ALL STUDENTS
General Studies
Tutorial
PE

STUDENTS CHOOSE FROM THE FOLLOWING - IN VARIOUS COMBINATIONS

'A' Level
Art
Biology
Chemistry
Computer Studies
Economics
English
Geography
History
Mathematics
Further Mathematics
French
German
Music
Physics

AS' Level
Economics

G.C.S.E. and other one-year courses
Art
Computing and IT
English
Foreign Language at Work
Geography
Graphic Communications
History
Mathematics
Modular Science
Pre-Vocational Studies
Welfare and Society

4

". . . courtesy and co-operation, enterprise and initiative . . ."

Form Tutors teach a tutorial programme which is designed principally to help students improve their study skills, develop their ability to understand themselves, the needs of those around them and the world outside. It is an important part of our curriculum and one which allows the form tutor, supported by a Head of Year, to spend time over a period of years monitoring the performance of students and working closely with their parents. In Upper School, the programme includes aspects of religious education and each year group meets regularly in assemblies that are broadly Christian in character. Social issues are always framed in the context of responsible, caring behaviour and with due regard to family and moral values.

Careers education begins formally in Year 9 and increases in prominence in Years 10 and 11 through the Tutorial and Modular programmes. All students have the opportunity to undertake a two week work experience as part of our well established careers provision which also includes work simulations, mock interviews, visits to careers conventions and access to a well stocked careers library and computer data-base. All this work is undertaken with the support of the County Careers Service, whose officers are in the school regularly.

We believe we are an outward-looking and forward-thinking school. We have many links with industry and commerce and a high degree of success in placing students in employment and in further and higher education, as is shown later in this prospectus.

We involve many other adults in the life and work of the school on campus and we take our students out on day visits, residential experiences, outdoor pursuits and to plays, concerts and lectures. We ask parents to make voluntary contributions to the cost of some activities; a full statement of our charging policy is available on request.

All students have individual educational needs; some need specialist help to stretch them, some need extra support to help them overcome their learning difficulties. Our Special Educational Needs Department concentrates on helping students master their difficulties to achieve good basic standards. The department works closely with outside agencies to ensure the most appropriate provision. All students must follow the National Curriculum and we aim to see to it that they do so at the appropriate pace and with the correct level of support. When learning difficulties occur, parents are always consulted at the earliest opportunity.

". . . the highest standards . . ."

Student Achievements and Destinations

One of our two libraries

Individual tutorial guidance in the Sixth Form

As the accompanying diagrams show, the majority of our students remain in full-time education beyond the age of 16, most of them staying on into our Sixth Form.

Similarly, the majority of our students in the Sixth Form take a full programme of 'A' Levels and then proceed to higher education institutions. The courses studied by them at universities, polytechnics and colleges of higher education cover a very wide range and in the past three years have included Medicine, Law, Engineering, Education, Business Studies, Modern Languages, English, Computing and Drama. Specialist courses are taken by

other students at Music and Art colleges. Our students enter many universities, polytechnics and colleges throughout the country, including six to Oxford and Cambridge universities in the past three years, and an increasing number are securing sponsorship from industry for their degree studies.

Of those who do not remain in full-time education, most enter employment locally, in areas such as banking, administration, retail work and management training. Others undertake courses of full-time professional training such as nursing or physiotherapy.

RECORD OF ACHIEVEMENT 1988-1990

This shows the destinations of our students on completion of their courses.

Fifth Year (Year 11) Destinations, 1988-1990

54%
2%
44%

■ 54% — Full-time education, H.G.H.S. Sixth Form (and further education)
■ 44% — Employment and training
□ 2% — Left the area.

Upper Sixth Destinations, 1988-1990

66%
28%
6 %

■ Universities
■ Employment
□ Further Education

66% — Universities, polytechnics and colleges for degree, H.N.D. and foundation courses.
28% — Employment and professional training.
6 % — Further education.

". . . commitment to the community . . ."

Community Provision

For many years we have been committed to working with and for the wider community of Harrogate. We have undertaken voluntary work of many kinds and have established many links with local industry. Over the last four years we have been working in partnership with Harrogate College of Arts and Technology, Harrogate Borough Council and others on a flourishing Community Programme. Taking place on the campus are many day-time and evening educational and recreational classes: the Granby Gateway Club for mentally handicapped adults meets weekly; numerous local sports clubs use our gyms, playing fields and swimming pool; a programme of sporting activities for all ages is run by the Department of Leisure and Amenity Services. We have a flourishing Youth Centre that has access to all our Campus facilities on three nights each week. Their activities are extensive and include: residential experiences, outdoor pursuits, dance and drama, information technology and voluntary work as well as the more traditional Youth Club activities.

At one end of the age spectrum our community provision accommodates a crèche and play group, at the other, a thriving 'Senior Citizen' Club and classes for the University of the Third Age. In every way we are a Community School and the daily presence of other individuals and groups on the Campus enriches the experiences of our full time students. These and other activities are all part of our commitment to the community of Harrogate. It is a partnership which we are constantly strengthening and developing and which at present brings some 5000 users on to our campus each week.

Extra-Curricular Activities

We offer many voluntary activities to our students, at lunch-times, after school and at week-ends. In addition, the normal timetable is suspended for three days at the end of the school year for Summer Activities, when students choose from a wide range of options: from rock climbing to writing a newspaper, from French cookery to a visit to London, and many more.

The pattern of extra-curricular activities varies from year to year but usually includes exchange visits to Europe, outdoor pursuits, the Duke of Edinburgh's Awards Scheme, skiing, theatre visits, computing and chess clubs, debates and various sports. Our reputation for musical excellence is well known. Our Concert Band is very much in demand at all kinds of functions and fulfils a busy programme of commitments, including overseas tours to Europe and North America. Our Chamber and Senior Choirs also give regular performances and compete in festivals in the area. The school orchestra and various ensembles give further opportunities for students to be involved in musical activities.

In drama, too, we have a strong tradition of major musical and dramatic productions and a recently opened drama studio is a very welcome addition to our facilitites. Excellent facilities are fully used for a range of sporting activities, including competitive matches against other schools.

On a residential outdoor pursuits visit to the Lake District

The school's indoor swimming pool, here being used by local primary school children

One of many extra-curricular music ensembles

" . . . excellent facilities . . . traditional values . . ."

A Partnership with Parents

To turn our curriculum planing into real and effective
learning requires parental support. We expect parents to
join us in a partnership which will benefit their children
throughout their years at Harrogate Granby High School.

Homework is set and marked by every department and
parents can check this through the 'homework diary'
which students must keep up to date. Parental support
helps students to keep their work organised and
completed on time.

We require that the correct uniform must be worn and we
assume that parents who choose our school, do so
knowing that we have this expectation and will ensure
that their children are always correctly dressed.

Similarly, we attach the greatest importance to courteous
and co-operative behaviour and if a student falls short of
our accepted mark then we employ a range of sanctions.
Parents are informed of all but the most trivial offences
and we feel sure that they will support us in demanding
the highest personal standards within our school
community.

Lower School Mathematics

Inevitably, difficulties do arise from time to time and we
are very pleased to discuss with parents any issues which
are causing concern. Details of the formal complaints
procedures are available from the school.

We do hope that you will develop a close relationship with
us, attending sports matches, plays and concerts and
supporting functions organised by the Parent Teacher
Association. We invite you to formal consultation evenings
to discuss your children's progress and written reports are
issued twice a year. Each half-term staff and students
produce a news-letter for parents called 'Granby News' to
report general news.

Un cours français

". . . outward-looking and forward-thinking . . ."

A Sixth Form student in the Information Technology Centre.

Upper School Technology

Transport

It is possible for students throughout the Harrogate district to travel to school by bus — from as far away as the northern outskirts of Leeds, Pateley Bridge and Knaresborough. Regular bus services arrive at the school from these areas and from all parts of Harrogate. The school regularly negotiates for new routes to be established so that all students who wish to attend the school may do so with ease.

Education for the 1990's and beyond

The school buildings date from the 1960's and stand in grounds which include 32 acres of playing fields. With departments based in suites of rooms, there are excellent facilities for all specialist subjects, including well equipped science laboratories and technology rooms, music practice rooms, four gymnasia, an all-weather pitch and an indoor swimming pool.

To keep pace with change we are continually striving to improve our resources and facilities.
The following are some of our recent and current projects:

— completion of the Business Education Centre, equipped with 22 Amstrad computers;
— completion of the Drama Studio adjacent to the music practice rooms;
— re-furbishment of the main library and resource centre;
— re-furbishment of the Sixth Form library;
— development of a new Sixth Form social area;
— completion of the Information Technology Centre in Lower School equipped with networked Nimbus work-stations;
— re-equipment of the languages laboratories.
— completion of a new Science and Technology Centre in Lower School.

We are committed to working for the highest standards in education in the 1990's and beyond. We look forward to welcoming you and your child into our school community.

The School Day

Our six period day begins at 8.50am and ends at 3.30pm, with a mid-morning break and a lunch break between 12.45pm and 1.40pm. Each period is 50 minutes.

Registration	Period 1	Period 2	Break	Period 3	Period 4	Lunch	Registration	Period 5	Period 6

School Year

1991/92	Sept	Oct	Dec	Jan	Feb	Mar	Apr	May		June	July
Closes		18th	19th		21st		10th	1st	22nd		22nd
Opens	2nd	28th		6th		2nd	27th	5th		1st	

In addition there will be the statutory five days of closure for staff training.

MAIN ROUTES TO HARROGATE GRANBY HIGH SCHOOL

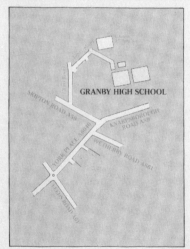

If, as a parent, you wish to know more about the school for your child's education . . .

If you are in business and would like to develop links with the school . . .

If you wish to find out more about the educational and recreational activities available through our community programme . . .

If you wish to use any of the school's facilities for recreational activities available through our community programme . . .

PLEASE WRITE OR TELEPHONE FOR FURTHER INFORMATION.

Harrogate Granby High School
Avondale Road
HARROGATE
HG1 4AR

Telephone: (0423) 564421

parents. It is obviously important to select the parents!
A promotional flyer should:

- be eye-catching and visually pleasing
- feature the school's name prominently
- include a contact address and map
- articulate the mission and strengths of the school
- use suitable vocabulary
- use good illustrations

It is likely that the overall quality of the flyer will be partly dependent on what other schools in the area are producing. Increasingly,
in the secondary sector, this means full colour photographs and a
glossy finish.

We reproduce in Figure 7.2 the flyer which is used by Granby
High School. Readers should note the way in which this has been
designed, making use of the photographs which had already been
taken for the main prospectus. The same messages are conveyed so
that the prospectus and flyer are seen as part of a coherent promotional strategy.

Distribution of Prospectuses, Brochures and Flyers

There is no point in producing this material unless someone is going
to read it! So what are the most effective ways of bringing the
documentation to the eyes of the client or prospective client?

We said earlier that governors, teaching staff, non-teaching staff,
pupils and parents are all ambassadors of the school but they can
only help if they realise that they are ambassadors and if they are
kept informed. Obviously, existing governors and staff need to have
an up-to-date prospectus if they are to represent the school. Prospective parents will also need to be given a copy. Existing parents will
receive an initial copy when their children join the school and may
only require a second copy when significant changes have been
made. When deciding where to place copies, the following
paragraphs may act as a useful reference list. Each school will have
to decide whether it is full prospectuses or shorter brochures and
flyers which are distributed in each case.

Primary or middle schools   The transfer of pupils from one phase of
education to the next provides the key recruitment point. Headteachers
and staff of these schools should be kept up-to-date about the secondary school and supplied with all the necessary prospectuses and other
material. This is obviously easier if the school deals with a limited
number of feeder/partner schools but the importance of regular com-

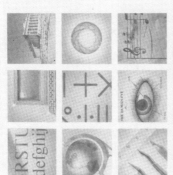
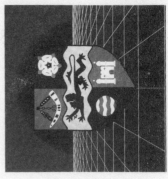
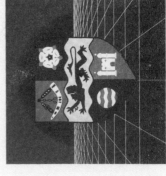

HARROGATE GRANBY HIGH SCHOOL

EDUCATION, INDUSTRY and the COMMUNITY – IN PARTNERSHIP

Harrogate Granby High School has strong links with many local employers, involving work experience placements, job shadowing schemes and various innovative curriculum-related projects.

An introduction to the Construction Industry – a careers event for our sixth form students by local industry (Walter G. Birch Ltd)

As part of its commitment to community education, the school has also developed a close partnership with Harrogate Borough Council's Department of Leisure and Amenity Services which runs a thriving recreation programme on the campus, sharing use of the school's facilities.

A work experience placement at Richard J. Eost Associates (Architects).

The school is now able to offer to local businesses, community groups and other organisations the use of conference and other facilities on the spacious campus, with easy access and excellent parking.

The school's indoor swimming pool, here being used by local primary school children.

Details are available from the school on request.

...CATION, INDUSTRY and the COMMUNITY – IN PARTNERSHIP

Listed below are just a few of the many local businesses and organisations with whom we have established close links:

Dunlopillo

OCTAVIUS ATKINSON AND SONS LTD

MASS...FIELD GROUP PLC

Walter G. Birch (Builders) Ltd.

MICHAEL DOBSON ASSOCIATES
CREATIVE SERVICES

Harrogate Borough Council Leisure Services

If, as a parent, you wish to know more about the school for your child's education...

If you are in business and would like to develop links with the school...

If you wish to find out more about the educational and recreational activities available through our community programme...

If you wish to hire any of the school's facilities for recreational, educational or business purposes...

PLEASE WRITE OR TELEPHONE FOR FURTHER INFORMATION

Harrogate Granby High School
Avondale Road
HARROGATE HG1 4AR
Telephone (0423) 564421

EDUCATION FOR THE 1990s

Figure 7.2 Harrogate Granby High School Flyer

... a hard-working and friendly community ...
... excellent facilities ...
... traditional values ...
... courtesy and co-operation, enterprise and initiative ...

We believe that we are an outward-looking and forward-thinking school, well equipped to meet the challenges of education in today's world. To keep pace with educational changes and developments such as the implementation of the National Curriculum — indeed, to set the pace in certain areas — we are continually working to improve our resources, facilities and professional expertise for the benefit of the students of this school and the people of Harrogate.

A-Level Physics practical lesson

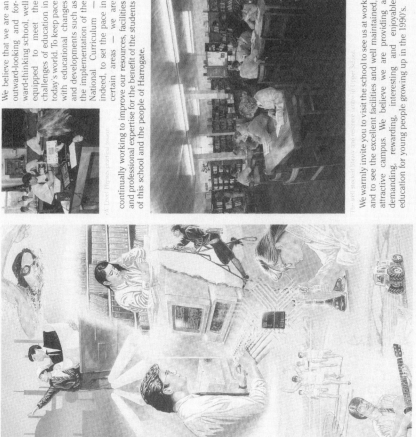

Lower school study area and resource section of Upper School

We warmly invite you to visit the school to see us at work and to see the excellent facilities well maintained, attractive campus. We believe we are providing a demanding, rewarding, interesting and enjoyable education for young people growing up in the 1990's.

EDUCATION FOR THE 1990's

WELCOME

Harrogate Granby High School is a hard-working and friendly community where achievements and relationships matter. All students are encouraged to develop their talents and interests to the full. We provide a well-structured environment in which the traditional values of courtesy and co-operation, enterprise and initiative are emphasised. We stress, too, the value of close, working partnerships — with parents, with industry, with the Careers and Youth Services, and with the community of Harrogate at large.

We are justifiably proud of the broad and balanced curriculum which is provided for all students and leads to examination results of which we can be equally proud. The majority of the students in our thriving Sixth Form study three or four 'A' Levels and most go on to universities, polytechnics or other higher education institutions.

Pupil uses Ecolonotes in their translation Workshop Centre

... developing talents to the full ...
... a broad and balanced curriculum ...

Figure 7.2 (cont).

munication, co-operation and information should be one of the top priorities in the marketing effort as the staff of these schools are often asked about a suitable secondary school by parents of pupils at the age of transfer. If such staff have several copies of a good quality prospectus it can convey positive messages about the secondary school at this critical decision time.

Citizens' Advice Bureaux   These bureaux can be a significant contact point for parents who are new to an area and who want information about local schools. They obviously need a stock of prospectuses and flyers to distribute as and when appropriate. For a list of the bureaux in your catchment area, you should write to the Citizens' Advice Bureaux, National Headquarters, Myddleton House, 105–123 Pentonville Road, London, Nl. If you discover that your school has been suggested by someone employed by the bureau, make sure that you thank the person responsible. This applies to anyone in any organisation through which a parent has heard about your school.

Public libraries   Most libraries now have an area where leaflets about local organisations or activities are displayed. The school's literature should feature in this section but it is also worth asking whether the staff are interested in having a copy of your school's prospectus in the reference section. Again this becomes a source of information to prospective parents making a choice about a school.

Estates agents and removal firms   Parents moving into an area will, in the first instance, contact estate agents for house details. If, at the same time, the agent can send them literature about local schools in the form of a flyer, then the initial contact will be made. The parents can then obtain information from the flyer and contact the school to request further details. While it may be too expensive to provide the agent with several hundred copies of the full prospectus, the provision of the same number of single A4 sheets or flyers is not. The estate agent could also be provided with a limited number of prospectuses to give out on request. It is important to maintain personal contacts with the agency staff, not only to keep them regularly supplied with the school's literature, but also to ensure that they themselves transmit positive messages about the school. It is also worth noting that some removal firms provide packs of information about an area and it would be worth checking whether they include information about local schools.

Information centres.   Many towns have information centres and it is important that they know about your school and have the relevant literature in case new parents to the area come and ask for it.

Doctors' and Dentists' waiting rooms   There are a number of places where
we sit and wait; doctors, dentists, health clinics, hospital out-
patients' departments, solicitors' offices etc. Instead of being faced with
the prospect of reading a six month old copy of *Woman's Own* or
Car Mechanics, up-to-date information about your school could be
placed in these areas. This will convey a picture of your school as it
currently operates and is a sound marketing approach within the local
community.

Local business firms   Local commercial and industrial firms should,
wherever possible, be given up-to-date copies of the school prospectus
and other information. This can be sent to the person who deals with
school – industry links and also to the personnel department which deals
with relocated staff. In this way, the school may recruit more pupils
but, more importantly, it will enhance its image so that industry links
and pupils' job opportunities are improved.

Local press and media   Local newspapers and local radio need to be
kept supplied with regular news information about the school, a point
which is developed later in this chapter. They need, in the first instance
to have reference material about the school and this can be obtained
from the prospectus. The school should therefore ensure that an up-
to-date copy is supplied to all local newspapers (including the 'free'
ones) and radio.

2   Other Written Material

If the school has spent a great deal of time and effort producing a
high quality prospectus it needs to ensure that the rest of its written
material reflects that quality approach. We have seen some professionally produced prospectuses which have inserts in the back
that have been run off on ink duplicators of indifferent quality. This
destroys the quality impression that has initially been created. The
school must therefore display a quality approach in all its material.
The type of material and the approach to be used is discussed in the
sections which follow.

(i)   Corporate identity

Most schools have some sort of logo, crest or other symbol of
corporate identity. This enables their documentation to be
recognised amongst others and helps to give a sense of 'belonging'
to the members of the school. Care should be taken to ensure that
the symbol is used in a consistent way every time. For example, it
should feature on headed notepaper but should also appear

somewhere, perhaps in a smaller form, on other printed materials. Large corporations in the business world spend a great deal of money on designing a corporate logo which conveys the right image and, above all, assists in recognition of the firm and its product. It is worth reflecting that they see great value in displaying a professionally designed, consistent image. Schools are not businesses but they do need to display some of the same corporate attributes.

(ii) General correspondence

All letters need to be produced on the school notepaper using a standard display system without any mistakes. The tone should be courteous and problem solving and not aggressive. This is easy to do when letters are produced for the senior management team by staff in the general office but it does require some effort to ensure that staff throughout the school use the same approach.

(iii) Information for job applicants

When information sheets are compiled for prospective job applicants they often comprise a collection of sheets produced by different people at different times. This can result in a lack of consistency which can give messages about the school and its organisation. There will probably be a covering letter, but all other sheets such as those which describe the school and those which focus on the particular post should be displayed in a similar style.

(iv) Newsletters

One of the minor, but recurring, complaints about schools is that they do not always communicate effectively with the parents and other clients. A newsletter is a popular way of attempting to bridge the gap between home and school. Unfortunately, there is still a lot of criticism about length, layout, frequency and content, even when the school has spent a lot of time and money on the production of the newsletter. Market research should have revealed information about the clients' preferences with regard to format that would enable the school to negate these criticisms and produce a properly targeted newsletter. Sometimes there may be a preference for an infrequent school newsletter but more regular year group sheets. Whatever the case, it would seem sensible to bear in mind the following points:

- it should not be too long — there is a tendency to stop reading after a few pages — one or two sides may be ideal because this avoids high costs and collation problems;

- it should be frequent enough to keep parents informed about activities but not so frequent as to become too ordinary;
- it must be easy to read — as with all written communications — this refers to the language and the layout;
- there should be an interesting layout — broken up by lists and diagrams;
- it is useful to apply some of the rules for prospectus design which are given on pages 90 to 92

While it may be a good idea to produce a newsletter and send it out with the pupils acting as the deliverers, most teachers know that there is no guarantee that it will ever reach home! Using a return slip which is signed by parents can be of great value in checking on delivery but can be frustrating for class teachers who have to collect the slips. Similarly, it may be a good strategy to send home written communications such as newsletters on the same day each week so that parents can be advised to ask that night for them. If the pupils feel that the newsletter is of value, then they are more likely to deliver it. This is another example of the importance of communicating to the internal market first.

(v) *Curriculum choice and option booklets*

Some schools take little care over information which they prepare for their existing pupils and for their parents. This attitude ignores the significance of the internal market. If it is an option booklet which is being produced, the subject staff must view the activity as one where they are marketing their subjects to the pupils. Even where subjects are compulsory, it is important for pupils to see them projected in a positive way so that they feel that a high quality product is going to be delivered. Teachers need to display a serious professional approach when dealing with this aspect of marketing if they expect a similar attitude from the pupils when they undertake the subject. Although most of the potential pupils are within the school, it may be that a school attracts pupils from outside because of the way in which it promotes its curriculum and option structure at the end of Key Stage 3. There is certainly considerable potential for recruitment from outside the school at the end of Key Stage 4. Schools will be in competition, not only with neighbouring schools, but also with Sixth Form Colleges and Colleges of Further Education. These competitors may be promoting a wider range of services and products than a school can provide so it is important to have done the market research and to put across a strong message which reflects client wants.

(vi) School reports

This is one item of information that all parents will read! The opportunity should not be lost therefore to produce a document which
enhances the school's image and reputation. This means that it must
convey useful information, rather than platitudes or brief words of
condemnation. Staff should understand the importance of
consistency of approach when compiling reports, especially if grades
are used. It is obviously important that reports should be free of
spelling mistakes and grammatical errors and senior staff should
establish monitoring systems in order to ensure that this objective is
achieved. Adequate time should be set aside for this important
means of communicating with the clients.

(vii) Letters about school visits

These form one of the most common communications between the
home and the school. However, as such letters are often produced
by a variety of departments, the standard of presentation and clarity
of explanation can vary considerably. There is an obvious need for
senior management to monitor these to ensure that the highest communication standards are being met.

(viii) Annual report to parents

The quality of these varies enormously from those which are dry
official documents to those which give an interesting account of the
school's activities. While the governors must meet the requirements
of the 1986 Education Act, the production of the document should
not be seen as a chore but more as an opportunity to get information
across and to promote a positive image about the school.

When looking at all the written material which the school sends
out the central factor is quality and, above all, consistent quality.
Good examples in one area of activity can be undone by poor
presentation in another. Managers in schools should strive to ensure
that different items sent out by different people in the school reflect
that quality and create a positive impression of the school. The
simple rules of clear language, easy to read, good display etc will
remain just rules unless there is that overriding commitment to
quality.

3. The Media

'Promoting the good news — limiting the damage of the bad'

Local and national media can be very significant in conveying messages, whether deliberately or accidentally. Schools must constantly be aware of this power, both in their direct dealings with the media and in their general day-to-day activities. Free publicity is very useful — if it is of the right kind! The school can build the use of media messages into its promotional strategies and can set up systems which will minimise the damage if any adverse messages reach the media concerning the school.

Although the full range of media are potentially available to schools, they vary in their significance and the way in which they might be used. National or regional television would be prohibitively expensive as an advertising medium but it could be possible to have the school featured in a programme. This is only likely to occur if the school has achieved something unusual which is of interest to the public at large. Recent experiments in local television may lead to a more appropriate means of communicating a school's purpose and activities to the immediate community. There is a similar pattern with other forms of media. Local radio may be more willing than national channels to feature the school in its programmes and the advertising slots will be more cost effective because they will be cheaper and more likely to reach the target clients. National newspapers are only likely to feature schools which have achieved 'firsts' of public interest or have achieved notoriety for some reason. On the other hand, the local press may be very willing to print material about a school. Most of the rest of this section applies to relations with the local press but could, if the circumstances arose, be applied to the other media.

We believe that there are two types of news — the good and the bad — and that, therefore, two approaches and sets of procedures are required. While it may be desirable to designate a member of staff who will liaise with the press on general matters, we believe that, when a problem arises and the media take an interest, then all dealings must be with the head or a nominated deputy. This person should be able to handle the situation sensitively because he or she has an overview of the issues and has experience in relating to the external environment in which the school exists.

It is important to develop a whole school policy for dealing with the good and the bad news and to communicate that policy by producing guidance for staff on all aspects of media links. Each partner in the school's activities, whether it is a member of staff, governor, pupil or parent, will then be aware of the possibilities and procedures. This will avoid a sparsity of coverage or, on the other hand, duplication of material and effort. The paragraphs which follow look at possible elements of a policy and set of procedures, using a simple division into the Who?, Why?, What?, When? of media links. We have not attempted to give a lot of detail about the operational aspects of the policy here but we would like to commend to the reader *'Public Relations and Marketing for Schools'* by Tim Devlin and Brian Knight (Longman 1990) which gives excellent coverage of these details.

Who? As indicated earlier, we believe that a policy should nominate those responsible for direct links with the media. In the case of bad news, this should be the head or a deputy. It should be made clear to all staff that, under no circumstances, do they make comments on behalf of the school, however innocent the question seems. At critical times it is important that a consistent balanced view is expressed and that the press are not given the opportunity to exploit a number of ill thought-out responses. It is always worth remembering that news-papers exist to sell copies and not necessarily to protect the reputation of schools! In the case of good news, a less senior member of staff is likely to be chosen to deal with the press. This may be the person who has overall responsibility for marketing the school, perhaps with a responsibility allowance attached, or it may be a different person who has an interest in this area. One aspect of this role is to ensure that there is coverage of a range of the school's activities to reflect the diversity of the educational experience and to appeal to a wide range of clients.

Why? The main reason for a media policy is to ensure a coordinated approach, enabling consistent, positive information to be transmitted to the media. A named person can build the links, coordinate press releases and ensure exposure by utilising their personal links and contacts. Thus the publication of good news can, like any other marketing strategy, enhance the school's reputation, advertise its events, recruit more pupils and generate resources in other ways.

What? Copy about the school's past or future activities can be supplied to the media. This should be relatively concise and should be compiled with some understanding of what will gain and retain the reader's interest. It is also possible for staff and pupils to be interviewed by journalists or presenters, but care should be taken here because the school has little control over what is published. There have been several examples nationally in which this type of relationship has been to the school's detriment.

The following list gives an idea of the topics which tend to be of interest to the public and hence to the media:

- sporting achievements
- academic achievements
- open days or evenings
- competition successes
- individuals' involvement in unusual activities
- visits and visitors, especially where overseas links are involved
- community involvement.

When?   The role of the person who liaises with the media is to ensure that there is regular coverage of the school in the local media without submitting so much material that there is overkill. Excessive publicity can give the impression that the school is only interested in activities which are newsworthy. It is obviously important to time publicity to coincide with school events and with the time at which choices of school are made by parents.

4. Advertising

Most of the indirect forms of advertising have been discussed in the preceding sections. As well as these indirect forms, many more schools are now turning to direct advertising in order to publicise their existence and their activities. Formal advertising may be in local newspapers or on local radio (television is prohibitively expensive and covers too wide an area) or by the use of notices at strategic spots in the local community or in local magazines/society newsletters. Schools already undertake a considerable amount of advertising but the scope has widened recently. Here are the various options for school advertising:

(i) Staff vacancies

This is the traditional form of advertising in which schools have been involved. They have used the national educational press such as the *Times Educational Supplement, Education* or the local press. Now that schools, rather than LEAs, are bearing the cost of these advertisements, they are identifying the target group more carefully and considering the cost effectiveness of the various newspapers and journals. If it is felt that a suitable candidate will be based locally, eg for a temporary post, then the local press is being used. On the other hand, when attempting to attract a high quality field for a senior post, the school is preparing an advert which gives a view of the school, rather than using the LEA general format. It is important to remember that the advert is not just about recruiting a member of staff but also about promoting the image and reputation of the school.

(ii)   School events   The advertising of school plays, summer fairs and other events helps to make the individual event viable but is also a wonderful opportunity to attract people inside the school and to display the work of the school to the wider group of clients. Local newspapers, radio, posters, flyers etc are all methods that would be used here. Care is needed if the event causes extra traffic and parking problems for the local neighbours otherwise there could be a dysfunctional effect on community relations.

(iii)   Pupil recruitment   Some schools use extensive advertising to attract new pupils but this has to be done in an ethical and appropriate way. It is common to publicise *open days* or *evenings* for prospective parents. The local press and local radio are the best media for this, especially if such an approach is backed up with leaflets for pupils in the feeder/partner primary schools. A variant on this is to advertise specific areas of the school, such as the Sixth Form, with lists of 'A' level options and past success rates. This could be because increasing the size of a school across all age groups is not always a good idea. It may be more appropriate to target specific year groups where the school can increase numbers through making existing group sizes more viable without incurring extra staffing costs.

Wherever advertising is used, it is important to remember certain rules:

- the advert should be attractive and eyecatching
- the advert should carry the school's name quite clearly
- if an event is being advertised the date and time should be included and any entrance fee (if appropriate)
- potential clients should be clear about how to respond, eg the venue for the event or how to contact the school for further details
- it should be tasteful and never, even by vague implication, disparage other schools

With these rules in mind schools should reconsider the use of advertising. If the cost of an advert results in a significant increase in the number of parents at an open evening, then the cost will be repaid many times over, especially if it is remembered that a new eleven year old pupil is in the school for the next seven years!

5. Word of Mouth

We have written about several ways of communicating so far which use modern methods for producing material that can project a positive image about the school. The oldest and still, in many respects, the most powerful is by word of mouth. The significance of this can be summed up by our belief that *'every school has a school gate mafia'*. This is not a problem for the school as long as it recognises that it has to *'manage the mafia in the interests of the school'*. This section is not taking a cynical view of communications by word of mouth but uses that example to demonstrate the power of the word of mouth and the importance of a proactive approach to managing such communications.

A good way of categorising these oral communications is to think of them as the four Ps those of:

- pupils
- parents
- professionals
- public

Assuming that these are the parents of the current pupils or those who have recently left, the first three of the Ps are part of the internal market. The importance of internal communications with these ambassadors was stressed at the beginning of this chapter. They are perceived by the general public as having an inside view and, therefore, the information which they pass on is perceived to be valid. They should be equipped with the right messages and with high quality materials which reflect the high quality product and service being provided by the school. One of the characteristics of the British personality is self deprecation and modesty; this is not always an advantage in marketing terms. More of the American viewpoint, exemplified by 'We are at the best school', is necessary if positive attitudes and messages are to be conveyed. A central task for school management is to decide how to encourage this type of attitude and pride in the school.

The first three Ps, it was stated, deal with the internal market. This is not completely true as one of them 'professionals' is also part of the external market. These are the headteachers and staff of feeder/partner schools. When faced with a choice of school in the future, parents will often consult the professionals whom they have come to trust and who best know the educational needs of the child. It is expected that fellow teachers will have an accurate view of the schools in the area. If such 'word of mouth' communications are to be to your school's advantage, it is important to ensure that all those who work in the feeder/partner schools have the same accurate information and positive views as the internal ambassadors.

The fourth P, the public, can be a very powerful determinant of the school's image in the community. If the 'public' begin to talk about the school in particularly complimentary or disparaging terms, the message soon spreads. It is important, therefore, to ensure that the message is a positive one.

When schools deal with people in all of these categories, and especially with the external market — the *public*, the way that the oral communication is transmitted and, more importantly, how it is perceived can be vital to the marketing effort. Similarly, when answering the telephone and dealing with requests to talk to the head, replies such as 'I don't know where the head is he/she is always wandering around somewhere' could be replaced with 'The headteacher is with pupils at this moment and always gives priority to pupil learning. Can he/she ring you back later?' This may have a better communication effect in terms of the school's reputation.

The way that other oral presentations and interactions at parents' meetings, open days and other events are carried out is significant in forming an impression of the school. This important area should not be ignored with the focus only being on written communications.

6. Other communications

There are many ways in which a school is engaged in conveying an image that enhances, or detracts from, its reputation. Some of these ways are not always apparent and it may be that the school does not recognise them or the significance of some of these methods because they are taken for granted and not seen as part of the promotion of the school. What follows is a discussion of several of these other methods of communication.

(i) School name

This, in itself, can convey an image of the school. It may be that the school wishes to appear to be traditional and long-established, thus it chooses to retain 'Grammar' in its title to build on the earlier reputation although it has become a comprehensive school. In the public eye 'Grant Maintained' may have associations with private schooling for some parents despite the fact that this type of school is a state school funded in another way. The inclusion of reference to the community reminds people that this is a community school or college with all that that entails in terms of access. Some schools feel that events in the past have damaged their reputations and a new name can suggest that things have changed. If this strategy is adopted, it is important to follow it up with *real* improvement.

(ii) *School signs and notices*

All too often, when visiting a new school it is difficult to find it. Tell tale signs appear, such as a flat roof or railings, but the sign can be small and overgrown by bushes! A school should be proud to proclaim itself to the community and this should be reflected in the school sign. It should be well designed and constructed, it should be easy to read by those passing the school, including motorists who have not been that way before. Traditionally, schools have been dependent on the LEA for signs and notices but in the era of delegated finance schools may find this freedom to design and display their own signs a useful advantage. If a school takes care over the appearance of its sign, there is a suggestion that similar care is taken over other aspects of the school. Also, in schools with a large campus or a split site there is a need for a number of signs strategically placed.

Once a visitor has found the school it is not always very easy to find one's way around. Finding the way to the secretary's office via the kitchens is not the best way to start a visit. Schools very often have clear signs from the front gate but not from where the visitor is coming — the car park! It is important that the signs and notices around the school should be clear and give adequate information. They should also be welcoming. Our most notorious example comes from the Midlands primary school which had on its gate 'parents not allowed beyond this point', perhaps not the most inspired marketing ploy! Unless they are for very short term use signs should be made of robust, wipeable materials. It is a good idea to ask a parent to walk round the school and to comment on the effectiveness of direction signs.

(iii) *Entrance hall*

All schools have cultures which are often reflected in their entrance halls. Some have honour boards and trophy cupboards while others have the 'drapes and driftwood' display so beloved in some primary schools. Whatever the preferred style it should be welcoming, well decorated, with displays of pupils' work and somewhere for the visitor to sit down. The reception area should be next to the general office and have easy and immediate access to it.

The way that people are received and where they are received leaves an important impression on them. One of the worst types of entrance hall is where there is a small sliding glass window where the visitor rings a bell, waits, and somebody puts their head through the window and says 'yes'! This is usually followed by the visitor asking to speak to a specific person, the window being closed again while the person is found and all the time the visitor is left in the entrance hall, sometimes with the added excitement of being there while the pupils go to break. This example is, unfortunately, all too prevalent. We talked earlier, in Chapter Two, of a client orientated culture — this is never more evident than in the way people are initially received. Staff training on how to handle visitors with 'good morning can I help you?' and not leaving them standing alone can be repaid many times over in terms of enhanced reputation for the school.

(iv)   Distinctive uniform

This can be a 'double-edged sword'. If it displays a high quality image, uniform can be a significant advantage. However, if the pupils are causing problems in the local fish and chip shop at lunchtime the advantage may not be so apparent. When we undertook a marketing day in a particular school one of the problems which the school articulated was concerned with location and uniform. There were three schools in the town, two on the fringes and this school in the middle. The two on the fringes had a similar burgundy uniform while this one in the centre had a royal blue one. At lunchtime pupils from the central school used the fast food and sweet shops in the town whilst those from the outlying schools were unable to reach them. It was not that the children at one school were any better or worse behaved than the ones on the fringes but they were considerably more noticeable if there was any trouble. Problems with misbehaviour in the town can be solved with strategies like shorter lunch breaks but changing the colour of the uniform to burgundy may be more effective! This type of analysis can also be applied to a school bus or minibus. If it is new, clean and the children inside it are well behaved then having the school name on the outside could be a positive advantage. If the opposite is true then the impact is very detrimental in marketing terms. (Putting a rival school's name on the bus is not very ethical!)

(v)   Use of school buildings/premises

There is no doubt that letting out school buildings can be a mixed blessing. Few, if any, events are economic if the income received is set against the fixed costs involved in the wear and tear of the buildings and equipment, rather than just against the marginal costs incurred in putting on the activity. Why then should schools be

E

involved in hiring out their premises to different groups in the community? It is a requirement that schools cover the direct costs of lettings; they cannot use the school budget to subsidise any external bodies.

Allowing different groups in the community to use the building for meetings or courses can have a considerable spin-off in marketing terms. This is very apparent in community schools which have additional budgets so that they can make wider educational provision for the community. Members of the community perceive the school to be theirs and forge links. They also see the school at first hand and have the opportunity to view displays of children's work. Many headteachers have little difficulty in convincing people of the worth of their school once they have got them through the door; the problem is getting them through the door in the first place. Use of the school by external groups is a positive way of building links to achieve this. There are also some key groups such as Brownies, Cubs and local primary school groups, the next generation of potential pupils, whose members can come into the school. Both the general enhancement of the school's reputation by expanding community links and the more specific forging of relationships with potential new pupils are activities which the school should encourage. The balance has always to be kept between this use and the way that it complements or detracts from the main educational activity.

(vi) Open days/evenings

These are significant events which can be advertised locally to bring different groups of people into the school. Traditionally open days have been for potential new pupils but they can also be targeted at different segments of the market. As well as new pupils the school could have a smaller open day targeted at local commerce and industry in which specific aspects of the schools' work can be illustrated and related in a much more direct way to their interests and needs. The same may be true of local residents and neighbours with which the school wishes to improve relations.

(vii) PTA and other parent events

These are a very significant way of involving parents in both supporting the school and of creating opportunities for parents to visit the school. By seeing the work of the school and interacting with the teaching staff, parents can have their decision to send their children to that school reinforced and reaffirmed.

(viii) *School cultural and sporting events*

The publicity value of school concerts, plays and successful sporting achievements has long been realised. The school has to ensure that it organises the communication with local press and media to fully exploit the opportunities created.

(ix) *Displays in the locality and displays in the school*

Inside the school one of the most positive images for visitors is displays of pupils' work. Schools that have long bare corridors not only create a dull environment but also miss a significant marketing opportunity. Outside the school, displaying pupils' work in local libraries, banks or building societies can be a good promotional approach.

(x) *Participation in competitions*

Like cultural and sporting events, quizzes, design projects and the like can provide opportunities to publicise and promote positive aspects of the life of the school.

(xi) *Industry links*

Building links with local commercial and industrial firms should be seen as a long term activity. The benefits can be in terms of work experience places for pupils, job prospects for school leavers and sponsorship. The blanket approach of writing to a large number of firms is usually ineffective. What is needed is a more personal and targeted approach where links are built up over a period of time to achieve mutual benefits.

(xii) *Video*

Few schools, as yet, have ventured into the production of their own video. Those that have tend to follow two courses. First are those made by pupils of the school showing aspects of school life for use with primary children about to transfer to secondary school. In that context they can be quite useful. Second are professionally produced videos that can be used with a much wider audience and which usually display a much higher quality of final product. The problem with the latter is that they can be very expensive. An interesting way to obtain a professional product at a reasonable cost is through the development of a joint project with students of media studies at a local institution of Further or Higher Education.

While we do not propose this is an exhaustive list of the ways in which the school can promote itself it does illustrate the possibilities available if a coordinated approach is used to exploit the opportunities that present themselves.

7. Group promotion

Many parents of primary age children may well be influenced in their choice of school not only by the reputation/quality of the primary school but also by the quality and continuity of education which that school can offer in conjunction with subsequent secondary schools. Several areas have developed 'pyramids' or 'families' of partner schools which formally develop this collaboration.

A significant area for development is, therefore, the concept of a group of schools coming together to market a package of education from four to eighteen. Provided that it is honoured, a promise of co-operation and continuity will attract parents and may even persuade some to 'opt in' from the private sector where such continuity is less common. 'Coherence and Progression' may be a good title for a joint promotional brochure!

Conclusion

This chapter has outlined a number of promotional techniques that are available. Schools should employ them to meet defined marketing needs and not as an end in themselves. It is too easy to be seduced into producing a new prospectus or writing press releases with glorious prose. With little time and few resources schools need to focus their activity to reap the maximum benefit from their efforts. To achieve this, the promotional techniques have to be part of developing and deploying a marketing strategy. The way in which they can be employed in this context will be considered in the next chapter.

8 Developing and deploying a marketing strategy

When all the earlier stages of the marketing cycle have been completed, the school should have a considerable amount of information from market research and from its review of the potential promotional approaches. There will have been a redefinition of the nature of the product and service which the school intends to offer and, at this stage, those with managerial responsibility for marketing will now be ready to decide how to set the promotional process into action.

This chapter is in a different style from earlier ones in that it integrates the text with a number of exercises to form a planning framework for a marketing strategy. The stages in this framework produce an action plan with the following sequence:

- Define marketing aims
- Find members for a marketing team
- Build a marketing team
- Set marketing objectives
- Prioritise marketing objectives
- Choose the promotional approaches
- Put plans into action

1. Define marketing aims

It is important to first consider the *aims* for this stage of the cycle. Is the school trying to achieve a general increase in levels of awareness about its purpose or activities or is there a more specific aspect of its work which needs to be communicated to a particular client group? Aims tend to cover broad areas and are not usually achieved within a short timescale. There should be some recognition of this so that instant results are not expected. It is unlikely that aims will be achieved at all unless the various partners in the school have been involved in their development and understand the reasons for them. Both the process of formulating marketing aims and the communication of these aims are important steps in the development of the marketing strategy.

EXERCISE ONE: DEFINING MARKETING AIMS

A. What are the aims of the marketing strategy?

B. How are the internal clients, in particular the staff, being made aware of these aims?

C. Do you have staff commitment to these aims?

---

2. Find members for a marketing team

Now that those responsible for the overall management of the school's marketing plan have stated in broad terms what has to be done, it is necessary to involve a wider group of people in order to divide up the work. This group will be particularly helpful when it is time to prepare and disseminate promotional material. However, in order to have commitment to the strategies, it is wise to involve this wider group at an early stage so that they can translate the marketing aims into objectives. A team, rather than an individual approach will be needed. This is to avoid too much work falling on too few people and, if carefully managed, it also helps to ensure a coherent message and a coordinated effort. When deciding who to involve, it is important to remember the broader client groups which were described in Chapter One. Involvement in the development and deployment of the marketing strategy will reinforce the messages which the school is anxious to communicate. The next exercise looks at the aspects of finding a team but it must be emphasised that the various partners in the school should be consulted about their possible roles, rather than have assumptions made about their preferences.

EXERCISE TWO: FINDING A MARKETING TEAM

A. Who is responsible for the overall marketing of your school?

B. Who could help to develop and deploy the marketing strategy?

Possible contribution

Governors
(you may wish to name them or to subdivide by type)

Teaching staff
(you may wish to name them or to subdivide in some way)

Non-teaching staff
- Clerical
- Technical
- Caretaking
- Cleaning
- Lunchtime supervisors

Regular visitors and helpers
(it is helpful to list the various types)

Current pupils
Year 7
Year 8 and 9
Year 10 and 11
Year 12 and 13

Current parents

Others, including the external clients (list types)

3. Build a marketing team

Once the managers of the marketing process have decided who will help with the marketing strategy, then it is worth spending some time building that group of people into a team. This will involve getting them together and ensuring that they all have a common view of the mission and aims of the school and that they all understand their role in developing and deploying the strategy which will communicate messages about the school to the wider group of clients. If the earlier stages in the marketing cycle have been carried out correctly, it is likely that many of this group will already have had some involvement. The following list of features of a team, as opposed to an ad hoc group, should help the managers to focus on issues which must be addressed at this stage:

- shares a common purpose
- plans the way in which it will operate
- uses the skills and knowledge of all its members
- recognises the contributions of all its members
- uses its time effectively
- works towards consensus
- has the full commitment of its members to any decisions
- makes decisions which can be implemented
- evaluates and improves the processes which it uses

EXERCISE THREE: BUILDING THE TEAM

A. List the people in the team.

When will the team first meet?

B. List the desired outcomes of that meeting.

The following may provide a starting point:

- team members should know each other
- team members should have an understanding of the marketing activities carried out so far
- team members should understand the aims of the marketing strategy
- team members should have a shared view of the team's role

C. What sort of activities must take place at that meeting in order to achieve each of the desired outcomes?

---

4. Set marketing objectives

Once the aims have been formulated and the team has been established, it is possible to move on to the setting of objectives. This should involve the team in taking an aim and agreeing the various objectives which must be met in order to achieve that aim. During this process each objective must be checked to ensure that it fulfils the criteria described on pages 81 to 82. Because of their specific nature, it is reasonable to develop objectives which will be achievable within one year. There will be ongoing monitoring and evaluation so that adjustments can be made or new objectives stated as time goes on.

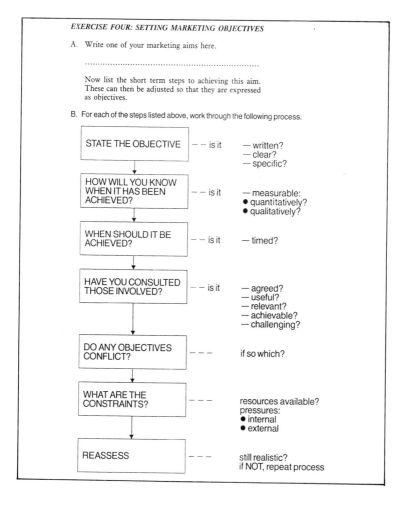

EXERCISE FOUR: SETTING MARKETING OBJECTIVES

A. Write one of your marketing aims here.

....

Now list the short term steps to achieving this aim. These can then be adjusted so that they are expressed as objectives.

B. For each of the steps listed above, work through the following process.

STATE THE OBJECTIVE	– – is it	— written? — clear? — specific?
HOW WILL YOU KNOW WHEN IT HAS BEEN ACHIEVED?	– – is it	— measurable: ● quantitatively? ● qualitatively?
WHEN SHOULD IT BE ACHIEVED?	– – is it	— timed?
HAVE YOU CONSULTED THOSE INVOLVED?	– – is it	— agreed? — useful? — relevant? — achievable? — challenging?
DO ANY OBJECTIVES CONFLICT?	– – –	if so which?
WHAT ARE THE CONSTRAINTS?	– – –	resources available? pressures: ● internal ● external
REASSESS	– – –	still realistic? if NOT, repeat process

5. Prioritise marketing objectives

If the process described in Exercise Four is followed for each aim, then it is likely that there will be a very long list of objectives which may appear daunting. The school should place these into some kind of order which will relate partly to priorities and partly to a natural grouping of activities. It is very important that the school should focus on three or four major activities such as a new prospectus, improved relations with the press and enhanced home – school links. This is because it is better to achieve these objectives rather than have an extensive list which, through pressure of work, would not be completed. The school year is quite clearly divided into terms so this may prove a good starting point for the grouping and prioritising of the objectives. The exercise which follows asks you to state the objectives for the whole year and then to focus down in order to establish priorities.

EXERCISE FIVE: PRIORITISING MARKETING OBJECTIVES

A. What are your objectives for this YEAR? List them and then mark them as A, B or C according to the urgency with which they must be achieved.

B. What are your objectives for this TERM. You will probably list all the category As from above but should also check whether any of the Bs must be achieved within this short timescale.

Add to the above list any objectives which should, for reasons of logistics, rather than urgency, be achieved during this term.

If you have included many Bs in this coming term, it may be that you are being over optimistic about what can be achieved.

C. What are your objectives for this MONTH? Mark against each the date by which it should be achieved.

6.   Choose the promotional approaches

The team will now have to devise a strategy for achieving the objectives within the planned timescale. Part of the role of the team should be to consider the promotional approaches which were described in Chapter Seven alongside the marketing objectives and to draw up a resource bid to senior management which will allow the marketing aims to be realised.

EXERCISE SIX: CHOOSING THE PROMOTIONAL APPROACHES

A.   Write down an objective or a group of linked objectives.

B.   Which promotional approaches are likely to offer the most effective means of achieving the objective(s)?

C.   Which resources are likely to be needed and what are they likely to cost in terms of materials, postage, labour?

D.   Indicate any resources which are available at no cost or any income which is likely to be generated if these approaches are used, for example voluntary help and advertising revenue.

E.   Summarise on one side of A4 the objectives to be achieved, the timescale, the preferred strategies and the resources which are required. It is essential to include the cost of the school staff, such as the office staff or technicians as they represent a real cost to the school.

---

7. Put plans into action

Once the general strategy has been approved and the resource level is clear, it is possible to deploy the marketing strategy. This will involve the team in deciding who does what, when and how so that all activities are carried out without duplication and so that they occur in the right order.

EXERCISE SEVEN: PUTTING PLANS INTO ACTION

The following chart can be used for a term or for the components of a task. When complete it sets out clearly what needs to be done, by whom and when. This is important so that members of the team and the school's managers are aware of what is happening. It also allows the project to be monitored to ensure that it is going according to plan or, if not, to enable plans to be modified where necessary.

Complete this chart for a term or component of the marketing strategy:

WEEK BEGINNING	TASK	NAME OF PERSON RESPONSIBLE	COMPLETED BY

Conclusion

These seven stages have described how a marketing strategy can be developed and deployed. It is important that the plans are realistic and focused. Achieving a limited number of objectives and building on them the following year is better than having a large number of half completed objectives. Marketing is a process that is ongoing and schools should not attempt too much in a rush of initial enthusiasm at the expense of a properly paced marketing strategy which will build up over a number of years.

9 Quality control of the education process

Promoting a school may result in a great deal of success in developing and improving the relationship between the school and its clients and may make a significant impact on recruitment levels. However, the initial success in these areas will be shortlived if clients are not subsequently delivered a quality product. Since the passing of the 1988 Education Reform Act a great deal of attention has been focused on delegated financial management and the consequent management skills and strategies which should be in place. However, this should not obscure the fundamental purpose of schools which is to promote effective learning by all the pupils. The evaluation of effective learning and, by necessity, the teaching that goes with it, has been the focus of traditional school evaluation. This evaluation needs to be reinforced by considerations of quality in all the school's activities in order to guarantee the best possible provision for the pupils.

Two perspectives can be employed here to ensure that this quality of provision to the clients is delivered. One is the traditional approach used in school evaluation in order to measure educational activity and the other is drawn from more recent considerations of quality control and quality assurance.

Traditional school education evaluation approaches

These have often been difficult approaches to use because of the lack of focus of the evaluation. It is important to be aware of what it is that is being evaluated; is it the inputs to the school, or its educational processes or some measures of outputs? This can be seen if we view a school as an organisation having inputs which are combined together through a process in order to achieve outputs as follows:

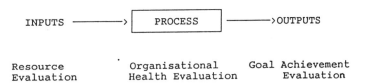

INPUTS ─────────> | PROCESS | ────────>OUTPUTS

Resource   Organisational   Goal Achievement
Evaluation   Health Evaluation   Evaluation

Evaluation can be carried out at any or all of these three points. The danger is that they are very often confused and individuals are unclear which form of evaluation is being used. To clarify this the reader can consider, for example, these three statements about inputs, processes and outputs:

1. The school has attracted 25 per cent of its pupils from outside the traditional catchment area.
2. The staff really work as a team in the school.
3. The school has achieved examination results 25 per cent better than the national average.

Each of these statements could be used in an evaluative sense and they represent input – process – output levels of evaluation respectively. The school must define the effectiveness concept which it wishes to explore and then to select the location (input – process – output or a combination) of the evaluation which will provide the most appropriate method for the school.

There have been several attempts to list performance indicators which a school should use in order to measure its effectiveness at any one of these three points. Operational problems have led many people to believe that an externally imposed model is unacceptable and does not produce valid, useful information on which to base school improvement. It has been suggested that the school might summarise its performance under the following headings:

1. Basic School Data — name, address, number on roll
2. School Context — sociocultural environment
3. Pupil Achievement — examination results
4. Parental Involvement — expectations and procedures
5. Pupil Attitudes — behaviour, homework patterns
6. Management — involvement of staff in policy formation, budgeting etc

These may be of considerable value when analysing a school's product from an educational perspective and, if used sensitively, they can feed information into the marketing process.

Quality control and assurance — concepts and perspectives

What is quality in education and how can we define it? This presents a difficult problem in looking at schools. Many commentators report that standards are falling and that quality is not as good as it was in the past, yet few attempts are made to establish quality standards which are recognisable and acceptable to a broad group of clients. The following are some definitions of assessing quality standards:

1. *Comparison with the past.* It is interesting that, in some areas of life, as with the purchase of a new car, comparisons are made with the future in terms of better specifications and standards of reliability than are currently available. People look to different specifications that will further improve quality in the next few years. In education, exactly the opposite is true. Past standards are often perceived as some sort of 'golden age' of educational excellence. The perception of grammar school education often has this aura of belief. The most significant example of a historic comparison is the change from 'O' level to GCSE examinations. The designing of a more appropriate, problem-solving and skills-based examination that will more closely meet the needs of pupils was criticised because more pupils passed than under the previous 'O' level system. If it was more appropriate, better designed and better taught then improved pass rates should be achieved but it was compared with an older, less appropriate, standard as a method of comparison. Thus, historical comparisons do have limitations in defining quality and should be treated carefully.

2. *Comparisons with other schools.* This can be a valid measure of quality if we are able to compare like with like, so that comparisons are made between schools with, for example, similar rolls, ability intakes, and facilities. Thus it is possible to compare the achievements of one age cohort of children in different institutions.

3. *Defining quality in terms of skills and competencies.* This involves setting predetermined levels of desired skills and competencies to be achieved by pupils. Monitoring the achievement level of pupils in these skills and competencies over a period of time then indicates improving or declining quality standards. This method has influenced several curricular innovations that have developed competency-based approaches. It also provides a significant tool for the school to define its own concept of quality.

4. *Level of quality needed for continued existence.* This can be interpreted as 'what is the minimum standard which a school has to offer its clients for them to continue to support the school?' This is obviously not a universal quality as schools will be in different positions regarding their clients. Some will be in a very competitive position vis-a-vis neighbouring schools while others will not, because of geographical location or selection criteria, have this element of market accountability. Similarly, the nature of the catchment area and the expectations of parents for their children will mean that some schools will have far greater expectations placed upon them by their clients so that they will be pressured to deliver higher levels of quality in their provision than other schools.

5. *Ultimate quality.* This is where a school sets targets based on a definition of an activity being 'as good as it could be'. Thus a perfect response to a client who telephoned in or the teaching of a perfect lesson would have characteristics ascribed to them and they would be goals to strive towards.

Schools need to set their own definition of quality and the standards which indicate that the desired quality has been achieved. The five definitions above provide a framework which a school can use to consider how it can develop its own most appropriate quality standard. This definition of quality not only applies to the teaching and learning process but to all parts of the organisation's activities. Thus, the way that the office staff respond to clients, the physical nature of the buildings, the attitude of staff towards pupils and parents, all display quality standards. Organisational structures and the nature and extent of staff involvement or participation in decision making can be indicators of a mature self-managing institution. Schools that are interested in the nature and dimensions of a quality institution could investigate the elements incorporated in *British Standard 5750*. This approach to quality monitoring and improvement, which sets criteria which must be met, is increasingly being used in Further and Higher Education. It makes a very significant contribution to this debate about quality.

It is a mistake to think that quality cannot be measured. It is not just an abstract concept which people debate but that cannot actually be put into practice. Quality can be measured by suitable performance indicators which have been developed from the aims and objectives of the organisation. However, performance indicators should not be misused; they are not in themselves measures. They are, as the name suggests, indications of whether performance is being achieved against specific targets. For example, academic 'A' level examination results might be one appropriate indication of teaching quality. However, if the majority of pupils had not followed this route but had undertaken vocational qualifications, the assessment of success would need to be made in the context of the overall pupil population within the school and of the appropriate goals which the school had set for itself in response to all the pupils' needs.

It is important that quality control should not be confused with quality assurance. Quality control is the way in which there is adequate monitoring to ensure that the minimum acceptable standards laid down by the school are maintained. As such they are a control and monitoring device and do not empower or enfranchise staff to gain ownership of the quality development process. Therefore it is much more important for schools to develop a programme of quality assurance. This is putting in place a system that will deliver high quality education in the future and act as a facilitating framework. Quality assurance can only be achieved if the head and other senior staff develop and operationalise strategies which support and encourage each individual within the school to achieve at the highest possible standard. To deliver this quality assurance school management has to:

1. provide confident, purposeful leadership that develops confidence and trust in the teachers so that they display high quality professional performance;
2. provide effective training and support that is necessary for the staff (teaching staff and support staff) to deliver a high quality product and service to the pupils;
3. relate a success culture (based on an organisational climate and ethos that focuses on delivering quality education) to appropriate goals which meet the needs of the pupils;
4. develop a learning environment for all individuals, staff and pupils, so that the mission statement applies to all the institution's members. The institution itself will then be a learning and growing organisation.

Conclusions

Putting these two concepts of evaluation and quality control/ assurance together provides a valuable perspective for management in schools. If clients are to be convinced of the quality of the institution itself and the education which it provides, then schools have to adopt a dual policy. They have to build on and develop their existing experience of evaluation of the curriculum and related activities but to extend that process into a much broader concept of quality control and assurance within the organisation.

Chapter nine: exercise one

DEFINING QUALITY

Take the five definitions of quality used in this chapter. Consider which provide the most appropriate framework to develop a definition of quality for your school.

1. Comparison with the past.

2. Comparisons with other schools.

3. Defining quality in terms of skills and competencies.

4. Level of quality needed for continued existence.

5. Ultimate quality.

Chapter nine: exercise two

QUALITY CONTROL AND MONITORING

A. In what ways do you monitor the quality of the teaching and learning process?

B. In what ways do you monitor the quality of the management support for the teaching and learning process?

C. In what ways are the administrative and support areas of the school's activity monitored to ensure that they are providing a quality service?

10 Monitoring the effectiveness of the marketing strategy

If a school is expending time and effort on the marketing of the institution, then it must ensure that the marketing effort has been focused and, above all, is having results. Just as a school evaluates its educational product to ensure that the educational aims and objectives which it set itself have been met, then it must also assess how far the aims and objectives of the marketing strategy have been achieved.

The monitoring process should be focused so that specific information can be obtained about how effective a particular marketing activity has been. If a more general attempt is made to evaluate the whole marketing process then it will be impossible to attribute the success to different elements and difficult to know which approaches to prioritise for maximum effect in the following year.

The monitoring of the effectiveness of the marketing strategy is built on the deployment of that strategy. These two elements can be seen to interact very closely. Once the marketing strategy has been developed two types of monitoring take place. Firstly, there is the monitoring of the implementation process and, secondly, the monitoring of the impact of that strategy. The first of these two monitoring processes is to check on the 'action' element in the marketing strategy; has the named person produced the necessary material or made the specified contacts or has the draft material come back from the printers? These are the sort of ongoing checking and monitoring activities that were suggested in Chapter Eight (Exercise Seven) and which need to precede an assessment of the effectiveness of the marketing strategy.

Many of the approaches and techniques outlined in the Market Research chapter (Chapter Four) can be employed to assess the effectiveness of the marketing strategy. The way in which they can be applied is seen in the following example.

Brentwich School, over a two or three year period, decides to target a number of marketing activities in order to improve aspects of the school's relationship with its clients. They are as follows:

1. The improvement of the open day/evening attendance by using better publicity to attract more prospective parents and prospective pupils to the event.
2. The production of a new, higher quality prospectus for promotional purposes.
3. The development of better quality advertisements and job specification material for new staff in order to increase recruitment.
4. The improvement of home/school communications.
5. The increasing of industrial/commercial links so as to enrich the curriculum and improve pupils' job prospects.

How can the school monitor and evaluate the effectiveness of its marketing effort in these areas? Firstly it is necessary to assume that the management structures and approaches outlined in Chapter Eight have been put into place and that the individual items form part of a coherent marketing strategy. Initially three basic questions have to be asked:

1. What did we plan to do?
2. What did we actually do?
3. What was its effect?

The first two stages define the precise scope and implementation of the strategy because if one element was missing then the effect of the marketing may be distorted and it is necessary to assess whether the particular strategy was ineffective or whether it was the implementation that was at fault. When these two initial stages have been completed the most important one, that of assessing the effect of the marketing strategy, can take place. To demonstrate the type of measures that can be used to assess the effect, each of the five examples will be analysed in turn.

1. The improvement of the open day/evening attendance by using better publicity to attract more prospective parents and prospective pupils to the event.

The obvious way to do this is to count the number of people who came! Obvious as it sounds many schools make generalisations about the number of people who attend and there is no specific attempt to calculate how many people came through the door. Similarly, it is important to find out where the people came from. Were they from an area where the school had targeted advertising so that it could be assumed that they had come in response to that? Or did they come from a different area for different reasons? Staff involved in the event should be asked to enquire about these factors. Similarly, staff should ask about what attracted prospective parents to the school and what they found valuable about the information they received at the open day. This sort of enquiry can be followed up through postal questionnaires to people who attended (if their addresses have been kept) or by personal communication when children are enrolled at the school. However, it may be that the parents who do not choose the school provide the more valuable information. This sort of research may not be necessary if the school takes the time and trouble to bring together all the information which individual members of staff have picked up during the day or evening. In the long term, the important assessment is, of course, whether more pupils attend the school as a result of this type of activity.

2. The production of a new, higher quality prospectus for promotional purposes.

It is quite easy to collect data on the number of requests for further details about the school or for visits to the school. It is, however, difficult to demonstrate a direct correlation between a new prospectus and any rise in such figures. Nevertheless, such data can help to feed into a wider information system regarding the value of the new prospectus. Office staff can be briefed to try, when they receive telephone calls, to gauge people's attitudes to the documentation which has been sent to them. New parents can be asked if the information is helpful and if the presentation is attractive, creating a positive response to the school and smoothing the transfer process for their children. Evidence can also be collected from staff as to whether the prospectus creates a positive image and pride in the school.

3. The development of better quality advertisements and job specification material for new staff in order to increase recruitment.

The type of criteria that could be used to assess the effectiveness of this would be to compare previous performance with the current position in a number of areas: the number of requests received for information and application forms, the number of application forms submitted, the quality of applicants and subsequent interviewees and, above all, the number of posts subsequently filled. This type of information provides very useful evidence of the success of the marketing effort in this area.

4.   The improvement of home/school communications.

A very good example of this was provided in Chapter Five which looked at the Cambridge Accountability Project questionnaire. Similarly, a random selection of parents can be telephoned on a regular basis to seek their opinions on the type and quality of information being received. Quantitative assessment of the number of parents returning reply slips or commenting on reports can indicate successful transmission of information and involvement.

5.   The increasing of industrial/commercial links so as to enrich the curriculum and improve pupils' job prospects.

There are various quantitative indicators which can be used to assess whether the marketing effort has had a result. These could include the number of links established, the number of firms that are prepared to take work experience pupils and the number of firms that will come into the school to assist in activities. Other assessments would include the amount of sponsorship, the reputation of school leavers and their ability to get jobs.

All these suggestions indicate ways in which the school can assess whether the marketing activities have been successful. It would be wrong to assume that evaluation is easy or that a perfect correlation between effort and result can be achieved. This should not prevent significant indicators being used as a guide for future action as long as they are interpreted in context and with sensitivity. Thus, evaluation is essential if the time, effort and resources allocated to marketing are to be well spent and to yield results. Schools must design their evaluation indicators to make an assessment which will guide the marketing strategy so as to maximise the results from their efforts.

Chapter ten: exercise one

MONITORING AND EVALUATION

A. List the marketing activities which were planned for the term/year.

B. Which were completed?

How was progress monitored?

What factors contributed to their completion according to plan?

C. Which were not completed?

Why were they not completed?

How can the situation be rectified?

Chapter ten: exercise two

EVALUATION OF THE IMPACT OF A MARKETING ACTIVITY

This exercise should be completed at the planning stage, not when an activity is complete.

A.   Which marketing activity is to be evaluated?

B.   When will the activity be completed?

     When will the evaluation take place?

     Who will carry out the evaluation?

C.   How will the evaluation be carried out?

     What success indicators can be established for the marketing activity?

11 Managing marketing in the 1990s

The most significant thing about marketing in the 1990s is that it is part of the integrated school development planning process. The elements of a school development plan are represented in Figure 11.1.

Figure 11.1 illustrates that providing for the three core areas cannot take place in isolation. It has to be done by integrating these core activities with the support and organisation functions. As can be seen, marketing is a major component in the School Development Plan and is an area which has to be addressed like all the other areas in the initial school development planning process rather than being seen as a 'bolt-on' activity or one which is undertaken when everything else has been done.

Therefore we strongly argue for the importance of seeing marketing as an integrated part of the School Development Plan. Having focused on a management approach to marketing in the book we put forward ten points for staff in schools to reflect upon when considering adopting and developing a marketing approach for their school in the 1990s. This is not put forward as a sequential number of activities but to act as a stimulus for discussion among senior management. When developing the marketing of their school, management should:

1. *Manage the introduction of a marketing approach in the school.* Like a number of innovations and changes in a school the chance of success may depend not necessarily on the context or the nature of the change but on how it is introduced. This illustrates the well known management maxim 'the way that you manage the change is as important as the change itself'.
2. *Market 'marketing' in the school.* Staff need to be convinced that marketing is an activity in which they need to be

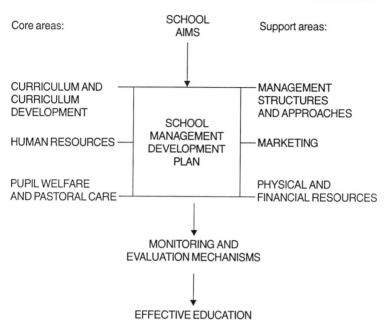

Figure 11.1 School development plan

involved. We should not be apologetic about marketing. For too long schools have been criticised by politicians and the media. We should take the initiative and put across positive images of the school. This can be done in an ethical as well as an effective way. Thus we need to positively sell the concept of marketing.

3. *Decide on the introduction approach — 'Big Bang' or 'Slow Creep'*. Does the school start developing a number of marketing initiatives and slowly involve different members of staff in this or does it attempt a major launch involving many staff. A whole school training day may be a suitable starting point for a new initiative on marketing.

4. *Note 'bolt-on' marketing to other activities*. Marketing should not be considered as an afterthought but as an integral part of an activity. The way that we communicate and promote the activities which the school undertakes should be a consideration at the design stage and not the implementation stage.

5. *Incorporate marketing into the school development planning process.* Short, medium and long term plans should involve a marketing strategy for managing the school's reputation and promoting its aims, goals and activities.

6. *Integrate marketing into the organisation's work and culture.* The staff of the school and the parents and pupils have to recognise, accept and believe in the significance and importance of marketing. This links back to the concept of them becoming 'ambassadors' of the school.

7. *Develop an outward facing and not an inward looking school.* Schools need to relate to the communities they serve and staff should look to taking the quality of what they do out to the market and promoting it. They must realise that it is their responsibility to change perceptions of the school in the wider world.

8. *Promote the concept and practice of the responsive school.* Schools should be market-orientated and not product-orientated; user-orientated and not provider-orientated; client-driven and not organisation-driven.

9. *Remember that 'First we make people and then we make things'.* This is a saying from the Japanese electronics industry but is just as applicable here. First we need to convince the people of the merits of marketing before we undertake the technical process of marketing the school.

10. Finally, *remember that marketing is a process and not an event.*

Concluding remarks

The central mission for schools is that they should provide the highest quality education possible. Nothing in this book suggests that this mission does not or should not remain as a central focus. We do not agree with the sometimes voiced criticisms of 'managerialism' that senior staff in schools of necessity become enamoured of the technical side of their management roles to the detriment of the effective monitoring of the teaching and learning process. Marketing therefore should not be considered as one of those management functions that only concern a few people and has little to do with the work of the school. It goes side by side with the educational process. If the school produces high quality education, marketing is the proud display of that quality. Communicating and promoting the school's aims and achievements also reinforces a positive image for those working inside the school. If the negative criticism of schools is to be countered and reversed, schools need to take the initiative and promote a positive view of themselves.

The book has outlined how this proactive management process can take place. This has to be within a marketing plan which involves a cycle of activities that form a process of marketing. We hope the reader will be able to apply the process to his/her own school to enhance its reputation.

Index